T0224075

Communications in Computer and Information Science   954

Commenced Publication in 2007
Founding and Former Series Editors:
Phoebe Chen, Alfredo Cuzzocrea, Xiaoyong Du, Orhun Kara, Ting Liu,
Dominik Ślęzak, and Xiaokang Yang

More information about this series at http://www.springer.com/series/7899

Jiajun Chen · Jiajun Zhang (Eds.)

Machine Translation

14th China Workshop, CWMT 2018
Wuyishan, China, October 25–26, 2018
Proceedings

 Springer

Editors
Jiajun Chen
Department of Computer Science
and Technology
Nanjing University
Nanjing, China

Jiajun Zhang
National Laboratory of Pattern Recognition
Chinese Academy of Sciences
Beijing, China

ISSN 1865-0929   ISSN 1865-0937   (electronic)
Communications in Computer and Information Science
ISBN 978-981-13-3082-7   ISBN 978-981-13-3083-4   (eBook)
https://doi.org/10.1007/978-981-13-3083-4

Library of Congress Control Number: 2018964092

This Springer imprint is published by the registered company Springer Nature Singapore Pte Ltd.
The registered company address is: 152 Beach Road, #21-01/04 Gateway East, Singapore 189721, Singapore

Preface

The China Workshop on Machine Translation (CWMT) brings together researchers and practitioners in the area of machine translation, providing a forum for those in academia and industry to exchange and promote the latest development in methodologies, resources, projects, and products, with a special emphasis on the languages in China.

The CWMT forums have been successfully held in Xiamen (2005, 2011), Beijing (2006, 2008, 2010), Harbin (2007), Nanjing (2009), Xian (2012), Kunming (2013), Macau (2014), Hefei (2015), Urumqi (2016), and Dalian (2017), featuring a variety of activities, including an Open Source Systems Development (2006), two Strategic Meetings (2010, 2012) and seven Machine Translation Evaluations (2007, 2008, 2009, 2011, 2013, 2015, 2017). These activities have made a substantial impact on advancing the research and development of machine translation in China. The workshop has been a highly productive forum for the progress of this area and considered as a leading and an important academic event in the natural language processing field in China.

This year, the 14th CWMT was held in Fujian, China, at Wuyi University. This workshop continued being the most important academic event dedicated to advancing machine translation research. It hosted the 8th Machine Translation Evaluation Campaign, featured two keynote speeches delivered by Rico Sennrich (University of Edinburgh) and Eneko Agirre (University of the Basque Country).

This year, the workshop focused on two hot topics, namely, simultaneous interpretation and low (zero)-resource machine translation. The first one is attracting increasing attention from industry. The second topic is very hot in academia and this technology is believed to solve the problem of low- or zero-resource language translation.

A total of 39 submissions (including 16 Chinese papers) were received for the main meeting. All the papers were carefully reviewed in a double-blind manner and each paper was evaluated by at least three members of an international scientific committee. From the submissions, 11 English papers were accepted. These papers address all aspects of machine translation, including named entity translation, knowledge graph usage, neural models, translation error analysis, and efficient MT system development.

We would like to express our thanks to every person and institution involved in the organization of this workshop, especially the members of the Program Committee, the Machine Translation Evaluation campaign, the invited speakers, the local organization team, our generous sponsors, and the organizations that supported and promoted the event. Last but not least, we greatly appreciate Springer for publishing the proceedings.

October 2018

Jiajun Chen
Jiajun Zhang

Organization

Honorary Chairs

Chengqing Zong	Institute of Automation, Chinese Academy of Sciences, China
Le Sun	Institute of Software, Chinese Academy of Sciences, China
Tiejun Zhao	Harbin Institute of Technology, China
Xiaodong Shi	Xiamen University, China

Conference Chair

Xiaodong Shi	Xiamen University, China

Program Co-chairs

Jiajun Chen	Nanjing University, China
Jiajun Zhang	Institute of Automation Chinese Academy of Sciences, China

MT Evaluation Chair

Shujian Huang	Nanjing University, China

Sponsorship Chair

Degen Huang	Dalian University of Technology, China

Publicity Chair

Yating Yang	Xinjiang Technical Institute of Physics and Chemistry, CAS, China

Program Committee

Hailong Cao	Harbin Institute of Technology, China
Wenhan Chao	Beihang University, China
Boxing Chen	Alibaba, China
Yidong Chen	Xiamen University, China
Yufeng Chen	Beijing Jiaotong University, China
Chenhui Chu	Osaka University, China
Chengcheng Ding	NICT, Japan
Jinhua Du	Dublin City University, Ireland
Xiangyu Duan	Soochow University, China
Chong Feng	Beijing Institute of Technology, China

Yang Feng	ICT/CA, China
Shengxiang Gao	Kunming University of Science and Technology, China
Yanqing He	ISTIC, China
Zhongjun He	Baidu, China
Rile Hu	shangque.com, China
Fei Huang	Alibaba, USA
Guoping Huang	Tecent AI lab, China
Shujian Huang	Nanjing University, China
Yves Lepage	Waseda University, Japan
Junhui Li	Soochow University, China
Maoxi Li	Jiangxi Normal University, China
Xiang Li	Xiaomi, China
Lemao Liu	Tecent AI Lab, China
Shujie Liu	Microsoft Research Asia
Yang Liu	Tsinghua University, China
Weihua Luo	Alibaba International Business Operations
Cunli Mao	Kunming University of Science and Technology, China
Toshiaki Nakazawa	University of Kyoto, Japan
Linfeng Song	University of Rochester, USA
Jinsong Su	Xiamen University, China
Zhaopeng Tu	Tencent AI Lab, China
Hasan Umar	Xianjiang University, China
Masao Utiyama	NICT, Japan
Mingxuan Wang	Tencent, China
Rui Wang	NICT, Japan
Zhiguo Wang	IBM Watson Research Center, USA
Fai Wong	University of Macau, China
Tong Xiao	Northeastern University, China
Hao Xiong	Baidu, China
Deyi Xiong	Soochow University, China
JinAn Xu	Beijing Jiaotong University, China
Kun Xu	IBM Watson Research Center, USA
Yating Yang	Xinjiang Technical Institute of Physics and Chemistry, CAS, China
Heng Yu	Alibaba, China
Dakun Zhang	Systran, France
Xiaojun Zhang	University of Stirling, UK
Feifei Zhai	Sogou, China

Local Organization Chair

Lei Guo	Wuyi University, China

Local Organization Co-chair

Yidong Chen	Xiamen University, China

Organizer

Chinese Information Processing Society of China

Co-organizers

Fujian Association for Artificial Intelligence

Wuyi University

Sponsors

Diamond Sponsor

KINGSOFT

Platinum Sponsors

Beijing Sogou Technology Development Co., Ltd.

Global Tone Communication Technology Co., Ltd.

Shenyang YaTrans Network Technology Co.,

Yunyi Technology Co., Ltd.

Tencent Technology Co., Ltd.

Gold Sponsor

Youdao

Silver Sponsor

Teksbotics

Teksbotics

Contents

A Grammatical Analysis on Machine Translation Errors

Shili Ge, Susu Wu, Xiaoxiao Chen[✉], and Rou Song

Guangdong University of Foreign Studies, Guangzhou 510420, China
gracekot@qq.com

Abstract. Machine translation errors are classified into groups of three grammatical levels: clause errors, clause-complex errors and textual errors, with a purpose to unravel causes leading to these errors. As illustrated with examples, clause complex presents different grammatical features from clause and the structural differences between Chinese and English at clause-complex level are the fundamental source of machine translation errors. This research, from perspectives of translation from Chinese to English and translation from English to Chinese, categorized clause-complex level structural differences between English and Chinese. The effects of these differences on machine translation are also analyzed, while future improvement suggestions on machine translation technology are provided accordingly.

Keywords: Error analysis · Machine translation · Clause complex
Naming-telling structure

1 Relation Between Levels of Meaning and Grammar

The fundamental task of machine translation (MT) is to translate the discourse of source language into the discourse of target language under the precept of preserving the original meaning. The discourse meaning, grammatically speaking, consists of lexical meaning and meaning existing among components relationships, which includes meaning existing among phrasal relations, argument relations, logical relations, reference relations. The grammatical system of a natural language can be classified into five levels: lexeme, word, phrase, clause, and clause complex (i.e., sentence with one or more clauses). Above clause complex is the highest level of discourse.

The above mentioned meaning is often relative to contexts, i.e. it has inherent ambiguity, which calls for a reasonable level of grammatical context to disambiguate. Regarding to ambiguity presented in lexical meaning or meaning existing among components relationships, if such ambiguity can be disambiguated at a certain level of context with human possessed knowledge, whereas the same ambiguity cannot be disambiguated at the next lower level of context, then the former level which helps with the disambiguation is marked as the grammatical level of meaning realization. In the case of machine translation, a failed disambiguation at the meaning realization level, i.e., an occurrence of a translation error, is classified as error at this grammatical level.

Take, for instance, the Chinese character "表" as an example. The character is inherently ambiguous in Chinese meaning by itself. As a noun, "表" refers to either a

J. Chen and J. Zhang (Eds.): CWMT 2018, CCIS 954, pp. 1–14, 2019.
https://doi.org/10.1007/978-981-13-3083-4_1

measuring tool of time or a form. In clauses "表走得很准。" (The watch is quite accurate.) and "表已经填好了。" (The form is filled up.), the meaning of "表" is disambiguated accordingly, with the first one meaning "a time measuring tool" and the second meaning "form". Suppose in such the clause, "你的表在桌子上。" (Your watch/form is on the table.), the character "表" is still ambiguous. If we supplement the clause with another clause, "已经修好了" (which is fixed), it is turned into a clause complex, and the ambiguity will be eliminated. The "表" here, refers to a time measuring tool. In a more complicated scenario, a clause complex, such as "你的表在桌子上，请你保管好。" (Your watch/form is on the table and you need keep it well.), the character, "表", still poses ambiguity. If there is another clause complex trailed after it, such as "这个表是一个证明文件，丢失了就麻烦了。" (This form is a documentary evidence and we will be in trouble if it is lost.), then based on these two clause complexes, the character, "表", in the first clause complex can be disambiguated in its actual meaning (i.e., forms). In these examples, the same character type of "表" occurs as different tokes in different contexts and the disambiguation of the character relies on different levels of grammatical contexts, which showcases relations between lexical meanings and its different grammatical levels. In the same way, the disambiguation of phrasal relations, argument relations, logical relations, and reference relations is also reliant on different levels of grammatical contexts. The relations of meaning and grammatical levels are illustrated as following Fig. 1. As seen in Fig. 1, different types of meanings can be revealed at different grammatical levels ("clause" as shown in Fig. 1 includes clause itself and levels below).

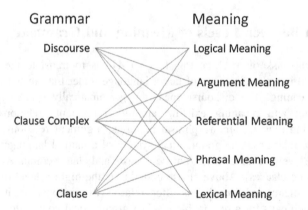

Fig. 1. Contextual relations at different grammatical levels.

Machine translation transfers from the source language, including lexical meaning and meanings among phrasal relations, reference relations, argument relations, and logical relations into their respective meanings in the target language. Such transformation of meanings is shown in Fig. 2.

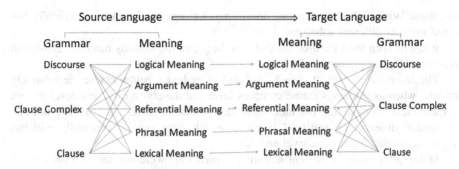

Fig. 2. Transformation of meaning in machine translation.

As illustrated in Fig. 2, in the process of translation, the transformed discourse maintains the original meaning but the grammatical levels of corresponding meaning related to contexts could be altered.

Ambiguity is one of the biggest difficulties for natural language understanding and processing. To analyze machine translation errors from the perspective of multiple grammatical levels can enlighten the way of machine translation improvement, which was hard to carry out in the past years but now it is possible and necessary due to the following reasons:

First, from the perspective of linguistic theory, it was not operationally clear for the differentiation of grammatical levels in authentic texts before. Especially in the case of sentence definition in Chinese language, only abstract descriptions are provided by grammar academics [1–3] and there are no operational theories or methods applicable in authentic texts processing, not to mention the study of clauses. In recent years, we have seen the construction of Chinese clause complex theory and corpus [4], and the construction of English-Chinese parallel corpus with clause alignment [5]. All these new development makes it possible to segment and analyze Chinese and English clause complex structure under the same theoretical framework, and compare and analyze the component relationships at the level of clause. Such progress offers a suitable theoretical framework and processing method for studying machine translation error at multiple levels.

Then, machine translation results were a messy group of words, leaving them impossible to be analyzed grammatically a few years ago. In recent years, machine translation has seen a significant improvement in its quality, especially with its fluency [6], which means generally, grammatical units can be recognized at different levels.

At last, even though machine translation has been improved greatly, it is still far from user's requirements. To further improve the quality, researchers have to evaluate translation results and provide feedback for MT researchers. The evaluation and feedback cannot be only a holistic score. Instead, a thorough diagnostic analysis into the translation results is a key process to classify the types of translation errors and discover their causes just as indicated by Wu et al. [7] that in MT quality estimation "the concrete error information in translation process has to be described". Errors occur at different grammatical levels, bounded by different contexts, and their grammatical mechanism is also different. Therefore, they need to be dealt with using different solutions. With such classification, future improvement can be more specifically targeted towards different solutions.

It can be seen from the analysis that it is the right time to study machine translation errors at different grammatical levels.

The linguistic studies at clause level and other levels below clause are relatively mature, whereas studies at clause complex level and the above discourse level are not yet sufficient. Considering machine translation errors, researches so far have not differentiated different grammatical levels at which error occurs, especially with no attention on clause complex level errors.

In the pilot study of present research, experiments were conducted with a small sample of English-Chinese and Chinese-English machine translated texts. The resulting statistics were presented regarding 3 types of errors: clause errors, clause complex errors, and discourse errors. As is shown in the results, the fewest errors are discourse errors and the ratio of clause complex errors to clause errors is 1:2. Thus, it is obvious that clause complex errors cannot be overlooked even though they are fewer than clause errors. The ratio indicates that serious effort has to be put into this field for future improvement of machine translation quality.

This research targets the observation of Chinese-English and English-Chinese machine translation errors at the clause complex level and analyzes the causes leading to these errors in order to provide a direction for improvement of machine translation.

2   Clause Complex and Naming-Telling Relations

Clause complex is a grammatical level above the clause level. Halliday and Matthiessen [8] indicate that "clauses are linked to one another by means of some kind of logico-semantic relation to form clause complexes." However, such a concept of clause complex is problematic in the study of Chinese because the definition of clause in Chinese language is not clear enough and logical relation analysis between clauses cannot be carried out. In order to delimit the boundaries of clause complexes and analyze the logical relations, naming-telling relations have to be determined with the delimitation of punctuations.

Naming is the starting point of discourse and telling is the explanatory statement of its naming

Example 1: 保定金末就建有 "万卷楼" 专藏经史, 并设有莲池书院, 曾为四方文人荟萃之处。 名胜古迹有古莲花池, 初建于唐高宗上元二年, 是中国北方古园林之一。

Example 1 has a period in between, but since the naming is shared by the period separated two parts, the two parts are included in one same clause complex. Therefore, Example 1 should be analyzed as follows:

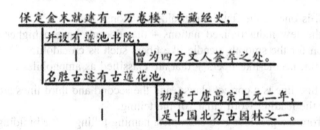

In Example 1, the indented lines are tellings, which are aligned with the corresponding right-side of their namings. Some namings do not start from the beginning of the naming line, which are termed as new-branch namings. A new-branch naming is marked by a vertical line to delimit its left boundary. Such analysis can cluster dispersed naming-telling parts together as below.

(1) 保定金末就建有"万卷楼"专藏经史,
(2) 保定 + 并设有莲池书院,
(3) 莲池书院 + 曾为四方文人荟萃之处。
(4) 保定 + 名胜古迹有古莲花池,
(5) 古莲花池 + 初建于唐高宗上元二年,
(6) 古莲花池 + 是中国北方古园林之一。

In the lines above, except for the second line, the naming and telling of each line can be joined into a correct Chinese clause. In the second line, the first word "并" of the telling is a coordination conjunction signaling the relation between clauses. Deleting the word "并", the second line is still a correct clause. By "correct", it means a subject-predicate structure with its components intact, accurate, and grammatically fluent in clause complex.

This same method can also be applied into analyzing English clause complex.

Example 2: The U.S. is one of the few industrialized nations that doesn't have a higher standard of regulation for the smooth, needle-like fibers such as crocidolite that are classified as amphiboles.

The naming-telling relation in English refers to subject-verb relation, also the relation between antecedent and its following explanatory components (attributive clause, non-finite verb phrase, declarative preposition phrase, postpositional adjective phrase, explanatory noun phrase (appositives, in most cases), etc.). All such relations can be illustrated with a newline indentation scheme:

The U.S. is one of the few industrialized nations

    | that doesn't have a higher standard of regulation for the smooth, needle-like fibers such as crocidolite

                                                   | that are classified as amphiboles.

Naming-telling relations can be clustered into the following groups:

(1) The U.S. is one of the few industrialized nations
(2) one of the few industrialized nations + that doesn't have a higher standard of regulation for the smooth, needle-like fibers such as crocidolite
(3) the smooth, needle-like fibers + that are classified as amphobiles

Here, the first line is a correct clause, and the second and third lines are correct, as well, without the leading word "that" of the telling.

As seen from the previous two examples, naming-telling is the building block of a clause. As seen from a syntactic-semantic relation perspective, naming is usually the argument of a certain components in the telling. At the same time, the clause, which is made up of naming and telling, is also the bearer of logic relations. All semantic relations on clause complex level including argument relations, logic relations, and semantic relations which need to be disambiguated at clause complex level, such as lexical meaning, phrasal relations, and referential relations, should be transferred completely with the original meaning during the process of translation.

3 Case Analysis of Machine Translation Errors at Clause Complex Level

This section provides Chinese-English and English-Chinese translation examples, illustrating the procedures of identifying machine translation errors at clause complex level with corresponding error types. The following translation examples were extracted from an online machine translation system, which is built upon the method of deep-learning technique, with translation output selected around May 20th, 2018.

3.1 Chinese-English Translation Errors

Human translation of Example 1

At the end of Jin, Baoding has built Wanjuan Building for collecting books on history. In Baoding there was a Lotus Pond Academy, where scholars from all walks of life gathered. There has being ancient lotus ponds, a historical site in Baoding, which were originally built in the second year of Shangyuan, Tang Emperor Gaozong and is one of the ancient gardens in Northern China.

Machine translation output:

At the end of Baoding, Jinding has built a history of the collection of Wan Wan Lou. It also has a Lotus Pond Academy, which was used as a place where scholars from all walks of life gathered. There are ancient lotus ponds, which were originally built in the second year of Tang Emperor Gaozong. It is one of the ancient gardens in Northern China.

The structure of this translation can be illustrated by a newline indentation scheme to present the clause complex naming-telling relation, with each line corresponding to the line in its original text.

1) At <u>the end of Baoding, Jinding</u> has built <u>a history of the collection</u> of <u>Wan Wan Lou</u>.

2) <u>It</u> also has a Lotus Pond Academy,

3) 　　　　　　　　　　　which was used as a place where scholars from all walks of life gathered.

4) <u>There are ...</u> ancient lotus ponds,

5) 　　　　　　　　　　　which were originally built in the <u>...</u> second year of Tang Emperor Gaozong.

6) <u>It</u> is one of the ancient gardens in Northern China.

In this scheme, the translation for the first line contains 3 errors: "保定金末" is translated as "the end of Baoding, Jinding", which is classified as proper name and phrase structure error. The verb phrase "专藏经史" is translated as "a history of the collection", which is classified as semantic and phrase structure error. And "万卷楼" is translated as "Wan Wan Lou", which is classified as proper name error. These errors can be found within clause by human without considering their wider contexts. Therefore, such errors are classified as errors within clause.

For the second line, the location of the verb "设有" in "并设有莲池书院" is translated into "it", which fails to clarify the exact location as specified in the original text. Therefore, it is a reference error. Since the location noun "保定" does not form an intact clause with the second line, this error is classified into a clause complex level reference error.

The translation of the third line is correct

In the translation of the fourth line, the translation of "名胜古迹" is missing, which is classified as error within clause; the translation output also fails to present the naming "保定", which is placed far ahead before a span of text consisting three punctuations. Thus this error is classified as an argument error at clause complex level.

The translation of the fifth line is missing "上元", an error within clause

The translation of the sixth line contains a word "it", which cannot serve as a clear reference to the naming "古莲花池". Thus this error is classified into an error at clause complex level.

In the translation output, errors within clause are marked with double underlines, and errors at clause complex level are marked with bold underline. This same marking scheme works for the following translations.

Example 3: 中国有5千年的悠久文化, 历史上最伟大的思想家是孔子。

(China has a 5,000-year-old culture and the greatest thinker in Chinese history is Confucius.)

Naming-telling relation is presented with newline indentation scheme

中国有5千年的悠久文化，

　　<u>历史上最伟大的思想家是孔子。</u>

Machine translation output:

China has a 5,000-year-old culture and the greatest thinker in <u>?</u> history is Confucius.

In the Chinese source text, the second line has an attribute "历史" and the attribute subject is "中国". Such a relation can be represented as a naming-sharing expression in Chinese; whereas, in English, such relation has to be presented with the attribute subject "中国" clearly stated in possessive noun form "Chinese history". The translation output does not present the subject separated by punctuation, which is an argument error at clause complex level.

Example 4: 他辗转联系上双峰县教育局, 了解到该教育局也在实行课程改革, 却苦于不知如何推动乡村学校改变。

(He contacted the Education Bureau of Shuangfeng County indirectly and learned that the Education Bureau was also implementing curriculum reforms, but was unaware of how to promote changes in rural schools.)

The naming-telling relation of this example is illustrated as follows:

<u>他辗转联系上双峰县教育局 ,</u>

<u>了解到该教育局也在实行课程改革 ,</u>

| 却苦于不知如何推动乡村学校改变。

The machine translation result is as follows:

He contacted the <u>Shuangfeng County Bureau of Education ...</u> and learned that the Education Bureau is also implementing curriculum reforms, but <u>he</u> is unaware of how to promote changes in rural schools.

In the first line, the English translation for "双峰县教育局" (Education Bureau of Shuangfeng County) is "Shuangfeng County Bureau of Education", which is a proper name error. The verb "辗转" is missing from the translation result, which is also an error at clause level.

In the third line, the naming should be "该教育局" (the Education Bureau), which was wrongly translated into "he", same to the "he" in the first line. This is a reference error and since the error occurs across punctuation, it is an error at clause complex level.

Example 5: 查伊璜心想: "我连吴六奇的名字也没听见过, 为什么送礼给我?" 当下沉吟不语。

(Cha Yihuang thought, " I haven't even heard of Wu Liuqi's name. Why did he give me a present? " He fell into a thoughtful silence then and there.)

The naming-telling relation for this example is illustrated as follows:

查伊璜心想：

　　　　"我连吴六奇的名字也没听见过，

　　　　　　　　为什么送礼给我？"

当下沉吟不语。

The machine translation output is as follows:

Chayihuang thought,

　　　　"I haven't even heard the name of Wu Liuqi.

　　　　why did you give me a present? "

?　the moment thoughtfully remained silent.

This is a super clause complex containing direct speech. The second line and the third line are direct speech, and the first line and the fourth line connect to construct into a whole discourse segment across the direct speech lines. In the third line, the agent of "送礼" should be "吴六奇", which is placed before the punctuation, and this "吴六奇" is translated as "you" by machine translation. Such an error is a reference error at clause complex level. The fourth line and the first line share the same "查伊璜" in Chinese, whereas English text cannot be translated with the same sharing relation. In the translation output, "remained" does not have a subject, which is classified as argument error at clause complex level. Besides, the person name "查伊璜" (Zha Yihuang) is translated wrong; the translation for "听说" is also wrong; and the translation for phrase "当下沉吟不语" is wrong, too. All these errors are identified within clause, which then classified as errors within clause.

3.2　English-Chinese Translation Errors

Example 6: They sow a row of male-fertile plants nearby, which then pollinate the male-sterile plants

For the source English text, the naming-telling relation is illustrated in newline indentation scheme:

They sow a row of male-fertile plants nearby,

　　　　　　　　　　　　which then pollinate the male-sterile plants.

The machine translation output is as follows:

他们在附近播种了一排雄性可育植物，

　　然后给雄性不育植物授粉。

In the second line of the English text, the antecedent naming is "male-fertile plants", but the machine translation output fails to translate "which", leading to the shared naming of "他们" from the first line to the second line, which then functions as the agent for "授粉" in the second line. Such an error is an argument error at clause complex level.

Example 7: The male part, the anthers of the plant, and the female, the pistils, of the same plant are within a fraction of an inch or even attached to each other

(雄性部分 (即植物的雄蕊) 和同一植物的雌性部分 (即雌蕊) 相距几分之一英寸甚至相互搭接。)

The naming-telling relation in English text is illustrated in newline indentation scheme as follows:

[The male part,
            |the anthers of the plant,
    and the female,
                |the pistils,
                 of the same plant]
                            |are within a fraction of an inch or even attached
to each other.

There are two parallel noun phrases placed in square brackets. These two noun phrases are combined together as a compound naming for the telling of the sixth line. At the same time, for each noun phrase, the head noun in each phrase carries its own appositive telling.

The machine translation output is as follows
同一植物的雄性部分,
植物的花药和雌性雌蕊在几分之一英寸内或者甚至相互连接。

In this translation, the compound naming of the noun phrase is wrong. The possible reason is that in the structure of "N1, A1, and N2, A2", the two nouns N1 and N2, carries its own apposition A1 and A2, respectively. Therefore, each noun phrase forms its own naming-telling relation. If considering their forms, it is easy to cluster N1, A1, and N2 as parallel nouns, which could lead to mistranslation. Such errors are argument errors at clause complex level.

Example 8: That's because pollination, while easy in corn because the carrier is wind, is more complex and involves insects as carriers in crops such as cotton.

(这是因为授粉虽然对玉米来说因媒介是风而容易, 但一般情况下是较为复杂的, 对于棉花之类的作物还涉及到昆虫作媒介。)

The naming-telling relation for the source text is illustrated in newline indentation scheme as follows:

That's because pollination,

> while easy in corn because the carrier is wind,
> is more complex
> and involves insects as carriers in crops such as cotton.

The machine translation output is as follows:

这是因为授粉是容易的 ，

因为载体是风 ，

玉米更加复杂 ，

并且昆虫作为棉花等农作物的载体。

The second line in the source text is an inserted logical subordinate clause. Such logical clause does not affect the meaning of the main structure (the first, third, and fourth line). It merely supplements the main structure with extra explanations. However, the machine translation did not provide such a differentiation. Instead, it follows adjacency principle, leading to the resulting associations of "pollination" and "easy", and "corn" and "complex". Such errors are logic relation errors occurred between clauses. So, they are classified into errors at clause complex level. Moreover, "carrier" is an ambiguous word here, which has several Chinese counterparts, such as "载体", "承运人", or "媒介". As in "because the carrier is wind", the word "carrier" is still ambiguous. But if considering the whole clause complex, since the topic is plant pollination, thus "carrier" can be translated into "媒介". Therefore, such an error is classified as semantic error at clause complex level.

4 Error Analysis at Clause Complex Level

Both Chinese-English and English-Chinese machine translation errors at clause complex level are mainly attributed to the clause complex level grammatical differences for the two languages. As discovered from this research, common causes leading to errors are as follows.

4.1 Chinese-English Translation

(1) Multiple tellings share one naming (see Example 1). Such instance is obvious in expository texts. For the purpose of explaining certain object or incidence, expositions from multiple aspects are often necessary, and even each aspect may need several sub-level expositions, as well. According to the writing style of Chinese text, the naming which is under explaining needs to be presented only once at the beginning of the discourse segment and its tellings can be placed far away from it. A period is often placed at the end of the exposition for one aspect,

which leads to the expansion of naming-telling relation across the punctuation of a period. As shown from statistics, in Chinese Encyclopedia texts, the number of periods which are transpassed by naming-telling relations takes up about 40% of total number of periods [4]. An English naming can only be followed by a few tellings. Thus, while being translated into Chinese, the shared naming in Chinese text has to be supplemented for each telling. In Chinese, the naming and telling are often placed afar and sometimes periods are placed in between, which makes it very difficult to supplement namings in machine translation. Most errors occur in such cases.

(2) The same naming may take up a different semantic role in case of matching different tellings (see Example 3). For Chinese, when a word functions as different argument roles, its form keeps the same and it often does not need any prepositions while in English this warrants a form change, leading to not only the supplementation of naming across several punctuation marks, but the form change of naming according to the argument requirement of telling on naming.

(3) The corresponding relation between naming and telling is paratactic (see Examples 4 and 5). In Chinese language, the naming of a certain telling could be most likely the subject of last main clause, but it also could be the verbal object, prepositional object, minor subject of S-V verb, subject of an object clause, etc. Their corresponding relations do not have any formal marks and are defined by meaning, i.e. "paratactic". For English language, grammatical marks are necessary so as to make such relations formally prominent. However, such grammatical marks could be placed in the wrong place in machine translation, leading to misrepresentation of naming-telling relations.

(4) A whole discourse segment separated by direct speech (see Example 5). English translation cannot match naming and telling across direct speech. Such cases are frequently seen in novels (especially traditional novels).

The probability of the last three cases is not large in Chinese language, but once such cases occur, the probability of wrong translation is high.

4.2   English-Chinese Translation

(1) Translation form choice of new branch naming-telling relations (see Example 6). The most common naming is subject and the most common new branch naming is verbal object or prepositional object. Among all namings in the two languages, more than 30% in English are new branch naming and only about 3% in Chinese [5]. Therefore, a large amount of new branch namings in English need to be transformed into different forms with different pragmatic functions when translated into Chinese. There are three ways of transformation: for most new branch namings, their tellings should be translated into the front positioned attributes for their namings; some new branch namings need to be repeated in other forms such as pronouns or nouns to form an independent clause together with tellings; a few new branch namings can still be shared as new branch namings and their tellings can be translated independently. As to which way should be chosen during translation, the decision depends on the semantic relation between new branch

namings and their tellings. Machine translation error is likely to occur under such circumstances and in fact, this is the most frequently occurred errors in English-Chinese machine translation at clause complex level.

(2) Two or more naming and its appositive telling co-occurrence in series (see Example 7). Usually the naming and its appositve tellings are both noun phrases. So, their relation can be easily misunderstood as a coordinate noun phrase relation. In English, appositive telling has a high frequency. Thus, these errors occur frequently as well.

(3) Multiple layer logic relations (see Example 8). In English, the logical expression of subordination can be presented as an independent adverbial clause or in the form of inserting a non-finite verb with logic conjunctions between subject and predicate. The latter form offers a weak logical meaning than an adverbial clause since it provides further explanations. Chinese also has such two forms of expression, but the latter form is restrained. Therefore, the latter form in English frequently causes errors in machine translation.

5   Conclusion

Machine translation between Chinese and English has shown a fast improvement of performance with deep-learning technology and multi-way supplementary methods. However, translation errors still occur frequently when translating complex sentences. To enhance the performance of machine translation systems and reduce the occurrence of errors, the discovery and pinpointing sources of errors have to be carried out so as to analyze the causes of errors. This question is studied in this research through grammatical analysis, classifying translation errors accordingly into three grammatical levels: within clause errors, errors at clause complex level and discourse level errors. Based on examples, the clause complex level presents different grammatical features from both clause level and levels below clause. The structural differences at clause complex level in the two languages are the major sources of machine translation errors. Regarding specific context of both Chinese-English and English-Chinese translation, this research lists major structural differences at clause complex level for these two languages, and it also explains the effects of such differences on machine translation. Owing to the larger context and longer distance of clause complex, the contextual semantic relations at such a level is a great challenge for machine translation technology to overcome so as to transfer the meaning of the source texts. Our analysis provides a clear direction for future improvement of machine translation technology.

Acknowledgement. This research is sponsored by the grant of National Natural Science Foundation No. 61672175, the 2016 Key Project of the National Languages Committee (ZDI135-30), and the Science and Technology Development Project of Guangdong Province, China (2017A020220002).

References

1. Zhao, Y.: A Grammar of Spoken Chinese. Translated by Lv, S. The Commercial Press, Beijing (1979)
2. Zhu, D.: The Lecture Notes of Grammar. The Commercial Press, Beijing (1982)
3. Shen, J.: On minor sentences and flowing sentences in Chinese: In commemoration of the 120th birthday of Yuen Ren Chao. Stud. Chin. Lang. 5, 403–415 (2012)
4. Song, R.: Clause complex and naming-telling structure in Chinese. In: Jie, C., Liu, M. (eds.) Frontiers of Empirical and Corpus Linguistics. China Social Sciences Press, Beijing (in press)
5. Ge, S., Song, R.: The naming sharing structure and its cognitive meaning in Chinese and English. In: Xiong, D., Duh, K., Agirre, E., Aranberri, N., Wang, H. (eds.) Proceedings of the 2nd Workshop on Semantics-Driven Machine Translation (SedMT 2016), pp. 13–21. Association for Computational Linguistics (ACL), Stroudsburg (2016)
6. Qin, Y.: An analytical study of neural network machine translation and its impacts on translation teaching. Technol. Enhanc. Foreign Lang. Educ. 4, 51–56 (2018)
7. Wu, H., Zhang, H., Li, J., Zhu, J., Yang, M., Li, S.: Training machine translation quality estimation model based on pseudo data. Acta Sci. Nat. Univ. Pekin. 54(2), 279–285 (2018)
8. Halliday, M.A.K., Matthiessen, C.: An Introduction to Functional Grammar, 3rd edn. Hodder Arnold, London (2004)

RST Discourse Parsing with Tree-Structured Neural Networks

Longyin Zhang, Cheng Sun, Xin Tan, and Fang Kong[(✉)]

Natural Language Processing Lab, School of Computer Science and Technology,
Soochow University, Suzhou, China
{lyzhang7, csun, xtan}@stu.suda.edu.cn,
kongfang@suda.edu.cn

Abstract. Discourse structure has a central role in several NLP tasks, such as document translation, text summarization and dialogue generation. Also, text-level discourse parsing is notoriously difficult for the long distance of discourse and deep structures of discourse trees. In this paper, we build a tree-structured neural network for RST discourse parsing. We also introduce two tracking LSTMs to store long-distance information of a document to strengthen the representations for sentences and the entire document. Experimental results show that our proposed method obtains comparable performance regarding standard discourse parsing evaluations when compared with state-of-the-art systems.

Keywords: Discourse parsing · RST-DT · Tree-structured LSTM

1 Introduction

A document is usually formed as a long sequence text and can also be analyzed as a constituency tree. The discourse tree can describe the organization of the document detailedly which is central to a number of NLP applications like sentiment analysis [1], text summarization [2] and document translation [3]. Rhetorical Structure Theory (RST) [4] is a representative linguistic theory of discourse structures, where a document is described as a discourse tree (DT), as shown in Fig. 1. Each leaf node of the tree corresponds to an Element Discourse Unit (EDU) which is also the smallest discourse unit (DU). Then, these leaf nodes are connected by rhetorical relations to form text spans recursively until the final tree is built. Each document unit is assigned a label (*nucleus* or *satellite*) about nuclearity according to the relation between this document unit and its siblings. The *nucleus* is the most important part of the relation and the *satellite* is less important. There are 78 fine-grained relations in RST, where some relations can only be either mono-nuclear (*satellite-nucleus*, *nucleus-satellite*) or multi-nuclear (*nucleus-nucleus*); some relations like *evaluation* can be either mono-nuclear or multi-nuclear according to specific situation.

The task of RST discourse parsing is to identify the relations between discourse units and to determine the structure of the whole document. This theory guided the annotation of the RST Discourse Treebank (RST-DT) [5]. However, the RST-DT discourse corpora are limited in size since annotation is time consuming and complex.

© Springer Nature Singapore Pte Ltd. 2019
J. Chen and J. Zhang (Eds.): CWMT 2018, CCIS 954, pp. 15–26, 2019.
https://doi.org/10.1007/978-981-13-3083-4_2

Due to the limitation of training data, most state-of-the-art approaches heavily rely on manual feature engineering [6–12]. While neural network models have been successfully implemented in many tasks, little neural network based RST-style discourse parser has been proposed up to now [13–15].

In this paper, we introduce a variant of the bottom-up tree-structured LSTM to better compute the representation for each text span based on the representations of its subtrees and the two trackers. We introduce two tracking LSTMs into our parser to store long-distance information which will be conducive to alleviating the problem of gradient vanishing. Compared with existing parsers, our parser can achieve competitive results. The rest of this paper is organized as follows: Sect. 2 is the related work, Sect. 3 will be our parsing model design, Sect. 4 the experiments, and Sect. 5 the conclusion and future work.

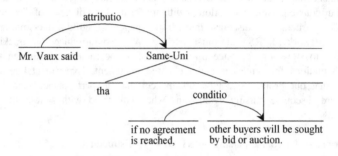

Fig. 1. An example of RST discourse structure

2   Related Work

The most previously proposed state-of-the-art approaches heavily rely on manual feature engineering. Hernault et al. [6] build a greedy model using SVM to transform this task into a labeling decision problem. Feng and Hirst [7] build a two-stage (sentence-level then document-level), greedy parser with linear-chain CRF models. The system proposed by Ji and Eisenstein [8] jointly learns the representation of the discourse units and a shift-reduce parser. Li et al. [12] propose to use dependency structures to represent the relations between EDUs.

Recently, some studies have focused on building neural network based discourse parser. Braud et al. [15] harmonize some existing corpora to leverage information by combining those data sets in different languages and use a feed-forward neural-network to score transition actions. Li et al. [14] use two bi-LSTM networks to represent EDUs and text spans separately. Li et al. [13] propose a recursive neural network model to compute the representation for each span recursively. However, recursive neural networks suffer from gradient vanishing as many documents are quite long sequences.

In this paper, our model is implemented as a shift-reduce discourse parser. For EDUs, we use an attention-based bi-LSTM to encode them. We introduce a variant of the bottom-up tree-structured LSTM to compute the representation for each text span based on the representations of its subtrees and the two trackers. The trackers we use are two simple sequence LSTMs that can store long-distance information to alleviate the problem of gradient vanishing. For transition action classification and relation classification, we introduce two separate classifiers to jointly train the model.

3 Parsing Model

Our method is implemented as a shift-reduce discourse parsing as described in Sect. 3.1. The method we use to encode each EDU is described in Sect. 3.2. We use a tree-structured LSTM to represent each text span and the *composition function* of our version is shown in Sect. 3.3. What's more, we introduce state tracker and connective tracker into this parser to supply an external input to this *composition function*, as detailed in Sect. 3.4. The two trackers can also supply features representations for the two classifiers we use in Sect. 3.5.

3.1 Background: Shift-Reduce Discourse Parsing

A shift-reduce discourse parser maintains two data structures: a stack S of partially completed subtrees and a buffer B of EDUs yet to be parsed. The parser is initialized with the stack empty and the buffer contains all EDUs $(e_1, e_2, \ldots, e_n)$ of the document in order. During parsing process, the parser consumes transitions $(a_1, a_2, \ldots, a_k, \ldots, a_{2n-1})$ constantly, where $a_k \in \{Shift, Reduce\}$. The state of buffer and stack will change according to the predicted action label. The shift-reduce parsing procedure is detailedly described in Table 1. When the buffer becomes empty and the stack has only one element, the shift-reduce process is ended. The last element in the stack is the target discourse constituency tree we need.

Table 1. The procedure of shift-reduce discourse parsing

Algorithm 1 Shift-reduce discourse parsing

> **Input:** EDUs of a discourse $[e_1, e_2, \ldots, e_n]$
> $state = [S, B] = [[\Theta], [e_1, e_2, \ldots, e_n]]$
> **while** B has more than 0 element **or** S has more than 1 element **do**
>> *action* = predict the action label by transition classifier according to the *state*
>> **if** *action* is $Shift$ **then**
>>> pop the first element b_0 from B and push it onto S
>> **else**
>>> pop the top two elements s_{-1} and s_{-2} from S
>>> capture long distance information i by tracking LSTMs
>>> $s_{parent} = composition\_function(s_{-1}, s_{-2}, i)$
>>> push s_{parent} onto S
>> **endif**
> **endwhile**
> pop the last element t from S
> **Output:** The target discourse constituency tree t

---

18   L. Zhang et al.

3.2   Representation for EDUs

Bi-LSTM and Self-attention. Bi-LSTM is a variant of recurrent neural network (RNN), it is meant to maintain a rough summary of the portion of the sentence has been processed so far. However, it only provides a final hidden state to represent the sentence which would be deficient as we need to capture some decisive local hidden states. Self-attention mechanism will put attention on all hidden states of a sequence and can extract relevant information of the sequence. It performs well on many tasks like natural language inference [16], text summarization [17], reading comprehension [18] and so on.

In RST discourse parsing, words at the beginning and the end of each EDU are decisive for transition prediction. Consequently, we introduce self-attention into this bi-LSTM based encoder with the purpose of obtaining decisive local information for discourse parsing, as shown in Fig. 2. We formulate the attention as:

$$a = [a_1, a_2, \ldots, a_t] = softmax\left(V_a \, tanh\left(W_a h^T\right)\right) \tag{1}$$

$$\vec{x}_{EDU\_encoded} = \sum\nolimits_{i=1}^{t} a_i h_i \tag{2}$$

where $h = [h_1, h_2, \ldots, h_t]$, $h_i \in \mathbb{R}^k$, $W_a \in \mathbb{R}^{n \times k}$, $V_a \in \mathbb{R}^n$ and both W_a and V_a are randomly initialized weights to learn.

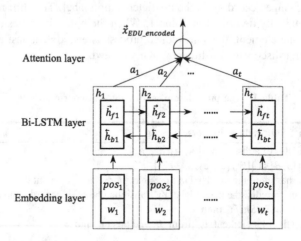

Fig. 2. Bi-LSTM & self-attention based EDUs encoder

Transformation. In order to better perform the calculation in the style of tree-structured LSTM, we use a learned linear transformation to map each encoded EDU $\vec{x}_{EDU\_encoded}$ into a vector pair $\left\langle \vec{h_b}, \, \vec{c_b} \right\rangle$ that stored in the buffer.

$$\begin{bmatrix} \vec{h_b} \\ \vec{c_b} \end{bmatrix} = W_{EDU}\vec{x}_{EDU\_encoded} + b_{EDU} \tag{3}$$

3.3 Composition Function

Figure 3 shows a variant of the bottom-up tree-structured LSTM [19], illustrating the input ($\vec{x}_t$), memory cell ($\vec{c}$) and hidden state ($\vec{h}$) at time t. It extends the sequence LSTM by splitting the previous state vector $\vec{h}_{t-1}$ into a left child's state vector $\vec{h}_{t-1}^L$ and a right child's state vector $\vec{h}_{t-1}^R$, splitting the previous cell vector $\vec{c}_{t-1}$ into $\vec{c}_{t-1}^L$ and $\vec{c}_{t-1}^R$. Different from other tree-structured LSTMs, we add an external input $\vec{x}_t$ into this model to solve the problem of gradient vanishing and the value of $\vec{x}_t$ comes from the two trackers we use in Sect. 3.4.

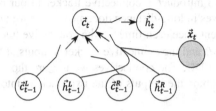

Fig. 3. Topology of tree-structured LSTM. Shaded node represents the input vectors from the two trackers. White nodes represent hidden state vectors and memory cell vectors.

When a *Reduce* action is performed, the representations of two text spans are popped from the stack and fed into a *composition function* which is also a neural network function that produces a representation for the new parent node at time t. The *composition function* calculates the parent node's cell vector $\vec{c}_t$ and state vector $\vec{h}_t$ as:

$$\vec{c}_t = \sum_{N \in \{L,R\}} \vec{f}_{t-1}^N \odot \vec{c}_{t-1}^N + \vec{i}_t \odot \left(W_{xg}\vec{x}_t + \sum_{N \in \{L,R\}} W_{hg}^N \vec{h}_{t-1}^N + b_g \right) \tag{4}$$

$$\vec{h}_t = \vec{o}_t \odot tanh(\vec{c}_t) \tag{5}$$

where $\vec{x}_t$ is an optional vector valued input argument which is either empty or comes from external sources like the two trackers (see Sect. 3.4), $\vec{f}_{t-1}^N$ is the forget gate, $\vec{i}_t$ is the input gate, $\vec{o}_t$ is the output gate, and $\odot$ is the elementwise product. The new vector pair $<\vec{h}_t, \vec{c}_t>$ that represents a new text span is then pushed onto the stack.

3.4   Trackers

Long Short-Term Memory (LSTM) network has been applied in many NLP tasks successfully for its ability to alleviate the problem of gradient vanishing and to provide long-distance dependencies. We introduce two trackers, and they are also simple sequence LSTMs, to store the long-distance information of a document.

During parsing time, our parser predicts a series of transition actions and relation labels according to the changing states (the stack and buffer). We use the first element of the buffer, $\vec{h}^0_{m\_b}$, and the top two elements of the stack, $\vec{h}^{-1}_{m\_s}$ and $\vec{h}^{-2}_{m\_s}$, to represent the state at the mth step. Different from other RST-style parsers, we take those changing states as a series of inputs to the state tracker [20], the input of which at the mth step is $state_m$.

$$state_m = \left[\vec{h}^0_{m\_b}; \vec{h}^{-1}_{m\_s}; \vec{h}^{-2}_{m\_s} \right] \tag{6}$$

Furthermore, we also introduce a connective tracker in our method to capture the information of connectives in long-distance documents. For we just need to track those connectives of a document once each time, so the connective tracker works only when the next transition is *Shift* and the connective tracker's inputs at the mth step are those connectives in the next EDU. The connectives we use are those artificially tagged in PDTB[1]. Finally, we combine the outputs of the two trackers into $h_{trackers}$, as shown in Fig. 4.

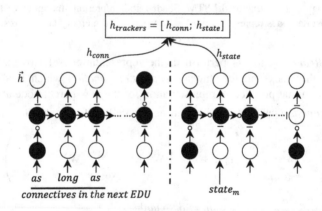

Fig. 4. Network architecture of two trackers we use. The left one is the connective tracker. The right one is the state tracker. We use two colors to reflect the switch of the LSTM gates.

---

[1] The Penn Discourse TreeBank 2.0. https://catalog.ldc.upenn.edu/LDC2008T05.

We use the two trackers in two purposes: the combined hidden state vector $h_{trackers}$ supplies a representation of the <*Stack, Buffer*> to the classifiers we use and it is also used as an input vector $\vec{x}_t$ for the *composition function* (see Sect. 3.3). With the use of the two trackers, the parser can compute the representation of text spans according to not only child nodes but also long-distance information of the document, which will alleviate the problem of gradient vanishing. Furthermore, better representation of text spans will supply more informative vectors for classifiers in turn which can directly determine the accuracy of the structure and relation.

3.5 Classifiers

Discourse relation classification and transition classification have different targets. The first one aims at predicting a perfect relation for two text spans and the later one aims at making a perfect prediction of which transition action to perform. Both these two classifiers can guide the construction of tree structures. For transition classifier, we construct 4 kinds of transition actions that contain Shift, Reduce-NN, Reduce-NS and Reduce-SN; for relation classifier, we use the 18 coarse-grained relationships in RST. The classifiers we use are detailedly described in Fig. 5. The tracking vector $h_{trackers}$ (see Sect. 3.4) is the input to the two classifiers. Meanwhile, many previous studies [6–8, 10, 11, 13, 14] have proven that the method of using handcrafted features is effective. Following their practice, we adopt some basic features they have used to strengthen our model. Here, we only care about the first EDU in the buffer and the top two text spans in the stack, and the features we use are listed in Table 2.

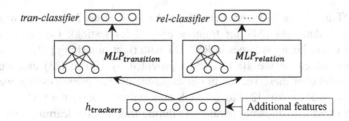

Fig. 5. Transition classifier and relation classifier

Table 2. Additional features

Features
Part-of-speech tags and words at the beginning and the end of the EDU
Number of words of each EDU
Number of words of each text span
Number of EDUs of each text span
Predicted relations of the two subtrees' roots
Whether each text span or both text spans are included in one sentence

In our view, the two classifiers we use both promote and repel with each other and the final goal is to achieve a balance between them. To achieve this goal, we assign each classifier a specific multilayer perceptron to get separate outputs y_{tran} and y_{rel}. The two classifiers will work separately to update the weights of two different multilayer perceptrons and work alternatively to update the shared parameters.

$$y_{tran} = softmax\left(W_{tran}\left[h_{trackers}; vector_{feature}\right] + b_{tran}\right) \tag{7}$$

$$y_{rel} = softmax\left(W_{rel}\left[h_{trackers}; vector_{feature}\right] + b_{rel}\right) \tag{8}$$

where $h_{trackers} \in \mathbb{R}^{l}$, $vector_{feature} \in \mathbb{R}^{m}$, $W_{tran} \in \mathbb{R}^{4\times(l+m)}$, $W_{rel} \in \mathbb{R}^{n_{rel}\times(l+m)}$, $b_{tran} \in \mathbb{R}^{4}$, $b_{rel} \in \mathbb{R}^{n_{rel}}$ and n_{rel} is the number of coarse-grained discourse relations.

4   Experiments

We evaluate our parser on RST Discourse Treebank (RST-DT) [5]. Since our work focus does not include EDU segmentation, we follow prior works and use manually segmented EDUs in RST-DT. For fair comparison, we apply the same setting on this to other discourse parsing systems and employ the same evaluation metrics defined by Marcu [21], i.e. the precision, recall, and F-score with respect to span, nuclearity and relation.

4.1   Experimental Setup

The RST-DT annotates 385 documents from the Wall Street Journal[2]. It was mainly divided into 2 data sets (347 for training and 38 for testing). Conventionally, we binarize those non-binary subtrees in RST-DT with right-branching [22]. We use word representation based on the 100D vectors provided by GloVe [23] and we do not update the weights of these vectors in our experiments. For preprocessing, we use the Stanford CoreNLP toolkit[3] [24] to get POS tags and preprocess the text.

We optimized the following parameters during training: the learning rate = 0.001, the dropout rate = 0.2, the batch size = 1 (document), the size of the beam $\in \{1, 2\}$, the size of POS embedding is 50, the size of connective vector is 64, the size of the hidden layer of tree-structured LSTM is 128 and the size of the hidden layer of bi-LSTM is 128. Our model was trained with RMSprop[4] to minimize two cross-entropy loss objectives with an l_2 regularization term where the regularization hyper-parameter is 10^{-5}. The final model was tested on the testing set after parameter tuning.

---

[2] https://www.wsj.com/.

[3] https://stanfordnlp.github.io/CoreNLP/.

[4] RMSprop is an unpublished, adaptive learning rate method proposed by Geoff Hinton.

4.2   Results and Analysis

We will show two groups of comparisons in this section to display the results of our experiments with respect to span (S), nuclearity (N) and relation (R).

Comparing with Other Systems. We compare our system with other state-of-the-art systems including Joty et al. [10], Ji and Eisenstein [8], Heilman and Sagae [11], Li et al. [12], Li et al. [13] and Li et al. [14]. Systems proposed by Joty et al. [10] and Heilman et al. [11] are based on variants of CRFs. Ji and Eisenstein [8] propose a shift-reduce parser that learns the representation of the discourse units and trains a SVM classifier jointly. Li et al. [12] propose a dependency parsing method and get a higher score in nuclearity than others. Li et al. [13] adopt a recursive deep model to deal with this task. Li et al. [14] propose an attention-based hierarchical neural network model along with some handcrafted additional features. We also report the scores of human agreement, computed and reported by Joty [25].

We divide these systems into systems based on traditional methods and neural network methods, as shown in Table 3. Compared with these systems, our proposed system outperforms others with respect to span and the scores of ours in nuclearity and relation are relatively lower than the corresponding best results. In general, our proposed method can achieve competitive scores when compared with most systems. By comparing the scores of systems based on traditional methods and neural network methods, we can draw an experimental conclusion that traditional methods perform better in nuclearity and relation detection, while neural network methods are better than traditional methods in span identification.

Table 3. Performance comparison with other state-of-the-art systems on RST-DT

System	S	N	R
Joty et al. [10]	82.7	68.4	55.7
Ji and Eisenstein [8]	82.1	71.1	**61.6**
Li et al. [12]	83.4	**73.8**	57.8
Heilman and Sagae [11]	83.5	68.1	55.1
Li et al. [13]	84.0	70.8	58.6
Li et al. [14]	85.8	71.1	58.9
Ours	**86.0**	70.9	58.1
Human	88.7	77.7	65.8

Comparing with Recursive Deep Model. Our proposed method is also a deep recursive model like the method proposed by Li et al. [13]. However, recursive neural networks suffer from gradient vanishing as the documents are quite long. In this paper, we aim at alleviating this problem by introducing two trackers which has been stated before. To strictly compare the performance of our method and the model proposed by Li et al. [13], we give experimental results that do not contain handcrafted features, as shown in Table 4. It shows that our proposed method achieves a better result in span and nuclearity compared with the model proposed by Li et al. [13].

Furthermore, we also give the experimental results when we do not provide the $h_{trackers}$ as an external input to the *composition function* (see Sect. 3.3). It shows that the overall performance of our system along with $h_{trackers}$ outperforms the system without $h_{trackers}$. So, we draw an experimental conclusion that the two trackers we use do provide long-distance information for structure building and transition action predicting. The results can also prove that our method has the ability to alleviate the problem of gradient vanishing when applying recursive deep models in RST-style discourse parsing.

Table 4. Performance comparison with recursive deep model

System	S	N	R
Li et al. [13] (no feature)	82.4	69.2	**56.8**
Ours (no feature, without $h_{trackers}$)	84.2	69.5	55.2
Ours (no feature)	**84.7**	**70.1**	56.0

5　Conclusion

In this paper, we propose a recursive deep model for shift-reduce discourse parsing. We introduce two tracking LSTMs as external inputs to the recursive model to alleviate the problem of gradient vanishing. Compared with most previously proposed methods, our shift-reduce discourse parsing system is competitive. However, our proposed method is a transition-based method which is relatively complex and we will try to simplify it in our future work. Further, we will focus on extending document-level structures to related tasks like discourse translation and discourse relation identification.

Acknowledgements. The authors would like to thank three anonymous reviewers for their comments on this paper. This research was supported by the General Program of the National Natural Science Foundation of China under Grant No. 61472264, the Artificial Intelligence Emergency Project under Grant No. 61751206, the sub-topic of the National Key Research and Development Program under Grant No. 2017YFB1002101, and the Young Scientists Fund of the National Natural Science Foundation of China under Grant No. 61502149.

References

1. Voll, K., Taboada, M.: Not all words are created equal: extracting semantic orientation as a function of adjective relevance. In: Orgun, M.A., Thornton, J. (eds.) AI 2007. LNCS, vol. 4830, pp. 337–346. Springer, Heidelberg (2007). https://doi.org/10.1007/978-3-540-76928-6_35
2. Louis, A., Joshi, A., Nenkova, A.: Discourse indicators for content selection in summarization. In: Proceedings of the 11th Annual Meeting of the Special Interest Group on Discourse and Dialogue, pp. 147–156. The University of Tokyo (2010)
3. Lin, R., Liu, S., Yang, M., Li, M., Zhou, M., Li, S.: Hierarchical recurrent neural network for document modeling. In: Proceedings of the 2015 Conference on Empirical Methods in Natural Language Processing, Lisbon, Portugal, pp. 899–907 (2015)

4. Mann, W.C., Thompson, S.A.: Rhetorical structure theory: toward a functional theory of text organization. Text-Interdisc. J. Study Discourse **8**(3), 243–281 (1988)
5. Carlson, L., Marcu, D.: Discourse tagging reference manual. ISI Technical report ISI-TR-545, 54: 56 (2001)
6. Hernault, H., Prendinger, H., Ishizuka, M.: HILDA: a discourse parser using support vector machine classification. Dialogue Discourse **1**(3) (2010)
7. Feng, V.W., Hirst, G.: A linear-time bottom-up discourse parser with constraints and post-editing. In: Proceedings of the 52nd Annual Meeting of the Association for Computational Linguistics, (Volume 1: Long Papers), pp. 1:511–1:521 (2014)
8. Ji, Y., Eisenstein, J.: Representation learning for text-level discourse parsing. In: Proceedings of the 52nd Annual Meeting of the Association for Computational Linguistics (Volume 1: Long Papers), pp. 1:13–1:24 (2014)
9. Marcu, D.: The rhetorical parsing of unrestricted texts: a surface-based approach. Comput. Linguist. **26**(3), 395–448 (2000)
10. Joty, S., Carenini, G., Ng, R., Mehdad, Y.: Combining intra- and multi-sentential rhetorical parsing for document-level discourse analysis. In: Proceedings of the 51st Annual Meeting of the Association for Computational Linguistics, Sofia, Bulgaria, pp. 486–496 (2013)
11. Heilman, M., Sagae, K.: Fast rhetorical structure theory discourse parsing. arXiv preprint arXiv:1505.02425 (2015)
12. Li, S., Wang, L., Cao, Z., Li, W.: Text-level discourse dependency parsing. In: Proceeding of the 52nd Annual Meeting of the Association for Computational Linguistics, Baltimore, Maryland, pp. 25–35 (2014)
13. Li, J., Li, R., Hovy, E.: Recursive deep models for discourse parsing. In: Proceedings of the 2014 Conference on Empirical Methods in Natural Language Processing, EMNLP, pp. 2061–2069 (2014)
14. Li, Q., Li, T., Chang, B.: Discourse parsing with attention-based hierarchical neural networks. In: Proceedings of the 2016 Conference on Empirical Methods in Natural Language Processing, Austin, Texas, pp. 362–371 (2016)
15. Braud, C., Coavoux, M., Søgaard, A.: Cross-lingual RST discourse parsing. arXiv preprint arXiv:1701.02946 (2017)
16. Parikh, A.P., Täckström, O., Das, D., et al.: A decomposable attention model for natural language inference. arXiv preprint arXiv:1606.01933 (2016)
17. Paulus, R., Xiong, C., Socher, R.: A deep reinforced model for abstractive summarization. arXiv preprint arXiv:1705.04304 (2017)
18. Cheng, J., Dong, L., Lapata, M.: Long short-term memory-networks for machine reading. arXiv preprint arXiv:1601.06733 (2016)
19. Zhu, X., Sobihani, P., Guo, H.: Long short-term memory over recursive structures. In: International Conference on Machine Learning, pp. 1604–1612 (2015)
20. Bowman, S.R., Gauthier, J., Rastogi, A., et al.: A fast unified model for parsing and sentence understanding. arXiv preprint arXiv:1603.06021 (2016)
21. Marcu, D.: The Theory and Practice of Discourse Parsing and Summarization. MIT Press, Cambridge (2000)
22. Sagae, K., Lavie, A.: A classifier-based parser with linear run-time complexity. In: Proceedings of the Ninth International Workshop on Parsing Technologies, IWPT, Vancouver, pp. 125–132 (2005)
23. Pennington, J., Socher, R., Manning, C.: GloVe: global vectors for word representation. In: Proceedings of the 2014 Conference on Empirical Methods in Natural Language Processing, EMNLP, pp. 1532–1543 (2014)

24. Manning, C.D., Surdeanu, M., Bauer, J., Finkel, J., Bethard, S.J., McClosky, D.: The Stanford CoreNLP natural language processing toolkit. In: Proceedings of the 52nd Annual Meeting of the Association for Computational Linguistics: System Demonstrations, pp. 55–60 (2014)
25. Joty, S., Carenini, G., Ng, R.T.: CODRA: a novel discriminative framework for rhetorical analysis. Comput. Linguist. **41**(3), 385–435 (2015)

Exploiting Knowledge Graph in Neural Machine Translation

Yu Lu[1,2(✉)], Jiajun Zhang[1,2], and Chengqing Zong[1,2,3]

[1] National Laboratory of Pattern Recognition, Institute of Automation, CAS,
Beijing, China
{yu.lu,jjzhang,cqzong}@nlpr.ia.ac.cn
[2] University of Chinese Academy of Sciences, Beijing, China
[3] CAS Center for Excellence in Brain Science and Intelligence Technology,
Beijing, China

Abstract. Neural machine translation (NMT) can achieve promising translation quality on resource-rich languages due to end-to-end learning. However, the widely-used NMT system only focuses on modeling the inner mapping from source to target without resorting to external knowledge. In this paper, we take English-Chinese translation as a case study to exploit the use of knowledge graph (KG) in NMT. The main idea is utilizing the entity relations in knowledge graph as constraints to enhance the connections between the source words and their translations. Specifically, we design two kinds of constraints. One is monolingual constraint that employs the entity relations in KG to augment the semantic representation of the source words. The other is bilingual constraint which enforces the entity relations between the source words to be shared by their translations. In this way, external knowledge can participate in the translation process and help to model semantic relationships between source and target words. Experimental results demonstrate that our method outperforms the state-of-the-art system.

Keywords: Neural machine translation · Knowledge-constrain
Knowledge graph

1 Introduction

With the rapid development of neural machine translation (NMT), we have witnessed the success of various NMT frameworks based on different neural network architectures such as recurrent neural network [2,13], convolutional neural network [7] and purely attention network [15]. Due to the powerful modeling capacity of these networks, promising translation quality can be achieved in several resource-rich language pairs. However, the conventional methods only focus on how to model the relationship between parallel sentences without resorting to any external knowledge (e.g. knowledge graph, KG). As a result, previous methods lack the ability to figure out the similar relations between (go, went) and (eat, ate). It is also incapable to tell the distinction between (king, man)

© Springer Nature Singapore Pte Ltd. 2019
J. Chen and J. Zhang (Eds.): CWMT 2018, CCIS 954, pp. 27–38, 2019.
https://doi.org/10.1007/978-981-13-3083-4_3

and (queen, women). Intuitively, the semantic relations between words should be maintained during translation while current methods cannot guarantee this.

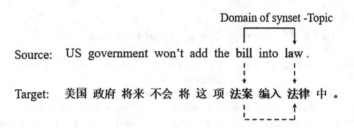

Fig. 1. An example of English-Chinese translation. The source word "bill" and "law" share the same relationship as the target ones

To address the above problem, we attempt to take advantage of the rich entity relations embodied in the knowledge graph to guide the translation process. The involving of KG strengthens the semantic relations between words and bridges rare words with common ones. We consider extracting multiple structured information from the existing knowledge graph to connect words with different relations. Since the knowledge in graph is distributed in various domains, including syntactic relations or other common-sense information, we can apply diverse knowledge to NMT.

We first extract from knowledge graph the triplets, consisting of a head word, a tail word and their relation, and then convert them to a computable format. To fully explore the usage of the knowledge graph in machine translation, we design two approaches using entity relations as constraints. One is monolingual constraint, which utilizes the entity relations to influence only the source side. Specifically, the monolingual constraint requires the embedding of the source words to hold the semantic relationship provided by the knowledge graph. The other is bilingual constraint that model relation equivalence between source words and their translations. Specifically, the bilingual constraint enforces the semantic relation between the source words should be exactly maintained by their corresponding translations. Figure 1 illustrates an example of English-Chinese translation. The relation between Chinese words 法案(bill) and 法律(law) in the target language should be the same as that between "bill" and "law" in the source language. Both of the monolingual and bilingual relation constrains are modeled during the training process and make the NMT system much more knowledgeable.

Due to availability of large-scale English knowledge graph, we perform English to Chinese translation task in the experiments to verify the effectiveness of our method. We expect the NMT training process would benefit a lot from the supplementary English KG under monolingual and bilingual constraints respectively. The extensive experimental results demonstrate that our method can outperform the state-of-the-art Transformer model in translation quality.

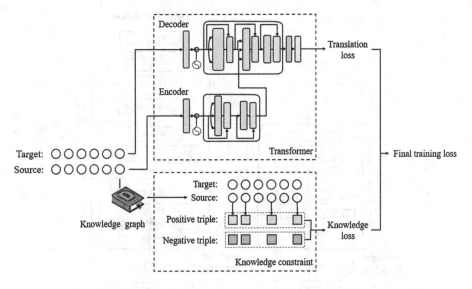

Fig. 2. The framework of our model. The Transformer part and knowledge constraint are independent before calculating final loss.

To further figure out how the external knowledge influences translation, we investigate whether the learned word embeddings really encode the semantic relations imposed by KG. Analogy prediction test is designed and implemented on the word embeddings. In this test, the head word and relation are given, our model selects the proper tail word from the candidate set. Compared to the baseline, our model has the ability of analogy and reasoning to some extent.

The main contributions of this paper are as follows:

- The knowledge graph is first applied in NMT to improve the translation quality.
- We design both monolingual and bilingual constraints to fully exploit the KG entity relations in the training procedure of NMT.
- The experiments on English-Chinese translation task show that both monolingual and bilingual constraints could achieve moderate improvements over the strong Transformer baseline.
- Our method significantly decreases the appearance of unknown words (UNK). The number of UNKs drops by 30.84% in NIST 2005 and the average reduction is 15% in other two test sets.

2   Neural Machine Translation

As shown in Fig. 2, our model poses knowledge constraint on word representations which can be implemented under various NMT architectures. In this paper, we utilize purely-attention transformer architecture which is shown in Fig. 3.

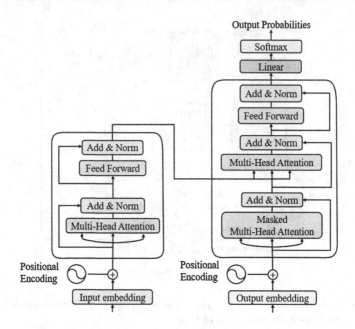

Fig. 3. The architecture of transformer.

Given the source sentence $X = \{x_1, x_2, ... x_n\}$ and the target one $Y = \{y_1, y_2, ... y_m\}$, this model abandons the idea of encoding successively and choose to operate self-attention mechanism over inputs repeatedly to obtain context information. Then, decoder also performs self-attention themselves and implement a multi-head attention upon the output of encoder to generate translations.

The encoder is a stack of six identical layers, each of which includes two sub-layers. A multi-head self-attention layer is set as the first sub-layer and a simple position-wise fully connected feed-forward network is the second one. Besides, a residual connection around each sub-layer is performed and followed by a normalization layer.

The decoder is also composed of six identical layers which have the same sub-layers as those in encoder. In addition, a multi-head attention over the encoder outputs is performed to help produce target translations.

Given the training parallel data $\left\{(X^{(z)}, Y^{(z)})\right\}_{z=1}^{Z}$, the final training loss function are all similarly defined as the conditional log-likelihood in despite of varied framework:

$$L(\theta) = -\frac{1}{Z} \sum_{z=1}^{Z} \sum_{i=1}^{m} logp\left(y_i^{(z)} | y_{<i}^{(z)}, x^z, \theta\right) \qquad (1)$$

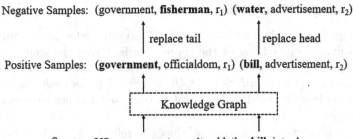

Fig. 4. An example of bilingual constraint. The source word "government" has relation r_1 with "officialdom" and "bill" has relation r_2 with "advertisement" in KG. We replace the head word "bill" and the tail one "officialdom" to construct negative samples.

3   Model Description

Similar to other NMT systems, the architecture mentioned above only concentrates on modeling inner mapping between parallel sentences. In this paper, we integrate entity relations, which are transformed to embedding constraint patterns independently, to strengthen the semantic relations between source and target words. In this section, we first introduce how to formalize embedding constraint on entity words. Then, two kinds of constraints, monolingual constraint and bilingual one, are designed to make knowledge assist training procedure.

3.1   Embedding Constraint for Relation Triples

We extract a set of fact triples, T, from knowledge graph. Each triplet is composed of a head word, a tail word and their relation. Referring to Lin et al. [9], we use embedding to denote the elements of triples which are mapped to the corresponding hyper space by mapping matrix as follows. The subtraction of the mapped entity vectors is forced to be close to the mapped relation vector. Specifically, the fact triple with relation r can be formulated as:

$$Tuple_r = (head, tail, r) \tag{2}$$

The entities and relation are mapped to embeddings, e_{head}, e_{tail} and e_r, and the following equation holds for each triple:

$$e_{head}M_r \approx e_{tail}M_r + e_r \tag{3}$$

where M_r is the mapping matrix which is specific to relation r. We score how well the elements of a triplet match each other by:

$$f_r(head, tail) = |e_{head}M_r + e_r - e_{tail}M_r| \tag{4}$$

3.2   Monolingual Constraint

In monolingual constraint, we only employ the entity relations to only influence the semantic embedding of the source words. Given the source sentence $X = \{x_1, x_2, ...x_n\}$, we extract the triples whose head word occurs in the source sentence, $S_{POS} = \{(head, tail, r)|h \in x, (h, tail, r) \in T\}$. For each positive triple in S_{pos}, we replace the head or tail word to construct the negative samples as $(head', tail', r)$.

As Fig. 4 illustrated, "government" has the relation r_1 with "officialdom" which is the out-of-sentence word. ("*government*", "*officialdom*", r_1) could be seen as positive sample and ("*government*", "*fisherman*", r_1) is constructed to be negative one by replacing tail word "officialdom" with "fisherman".

Instead of random replacement which may introduce false negative labels, we choose to select replacement by probabilities. A different sampling method in Wang et al. [16] is adapted where the head entity is more likely to be swapped if the relation is one-to-many.

The loss function of monolingual constraint can be written as:

$$L(x^{(z)}, y^{(z)}) = \frac{1}{N} \sum_{(head, tail, r) \in S_{pos}} max(0, f_r(head, tail) + \gamma - f_r(head', tail')) \quad (5)$$

where N denotes the number of positive samples and γ is the hyper parameter.

3.3   Bilingual Constraint

In bilingual constraint, we reckon that the relation between source entities should be maintained by their translations. We first extract all triples, whose head and tail words both appear in source sentence, $S_{src} = \{(head_{src}, tail_{src}, r)|head_{src} \in x, tail_{src} \in x\}$. Then we align the head and tail words of triples in S_{src} to their translations as $S_{tar} = \{(head_{tar}, tail_{tar}, r)|head_{tar} \in y, tail_{tar} \in y\}$. To minimize the gap between source triplet and aligned target one, the loss function can be set as:

$$L(x^{(z)}, y^{(z)}) = -\frac{1}{N} \sum_{(head_{src}, tail_{src}, r) \in S_{pos}} |f_r(head_{src}, tail_{src}) - f_r(head_{tar}, tail_{tar})| \quad (6)$$

3.4   Adding Constraint in NMT

Monolingual or bilingual constraints are used to improve semantic word embeddings during NMT training. As shown in Fig. 2, the overall loss functions mainly includes two parts: one is from conventional translation and the other is from the entity relation loss:

$$Loss = \frac{1}{Z} \sum_{z=1}^{Z} \sum_{i=1}^{m} log\left(y_i^{(z)}|y_{<i}^{(z)}, x^z, \theta\right) + \alpha \frac{1}{Z} \sum_{z=1}^{Z} L(x^{(z)}, y^{(z)}) + \beta ||M_r||^2 \quad (7)$$

where α, β are hyper parameters and $||M_r||^2$ is set as regularization. In practice, the translation loss and the entity relation loss are optimized iteratively.

4 Experiments

4.1 Dataset

We conduct our experiments on the NIST English-Chinese translation task since there are plenty of knowledge graphs in English. Due to absence of multiple test sets for English-Chinese translation, we construct the test sets from the original NIST Chinese-English dataset in which each Chinese source sentence has four English references. For each instance, we regard first English reference as source sentence and the Chinese sentence as single reference. The evaluation metric is BLEU [12] and we select the character-based BLEU-5 which is suitable for Chinese.

Our training data consists of 2.1M sentences pair. Besides, NIST 2002 dataset and NIST 2005, 2006 and 2008 datasets are selected as our development and test sets, respectively.

For knowledge extraction, we filter triples from Wordnet covering 155K entities and 27 relationships. So as to obtain high-quality triples, we discard some low-frequency relations and dual triples where exchange of head and tail words makes no difference. The final fact triple extraction covers 11 relations, which is utilized to match entities in source and target sentences. In monolingual case, the average matching number of one sentence is 7.54 triples. While in bilingual case, the triples where head and tail entities are both lying in source sentence are selected and Fast Align [6] is used to match target side words. However, because of low matching ratio of bilingual situation, we only make our bilingual experiments on 250K pairs of sentences which cover matched entities.

As for analogy prediction test, we extract 1K triples from Wordnet and arbitrarily select another four words for each triple as tail word candidates. We also have to ensure that the given head word, relation and five tail word candidates are contained in dictionaries.

4.2 Training Details

We perform all the experiments using Tensor2tensor, an open-source tool provided by Google. The settings of the training procedure and the hyper parameters are similar to "transformer big single GPU" mode in Tensor2tensor. In detail, we set batch size as 1024, hidden layer as 512 and training step as 300K. We limit the vocabularies to the words whose frequencies are more than 20 and also construct relation vocabulary covering 11 relations. During training, we set hyper parameters α among $\{0.035, 0.06, 0.1, 0.2\}$, β among $\{0.0001, 0.001, 0.002, 0.006\}$ for monolingual constraint. In bilingual constraint, we select α among $\{0.5, 1, 1.5, 2\}$, β among $\{0.035, 0.07, 0.105, 0.15\}$, γ is set to 10.

4.3 Results on English-Chinese Translation

Monolingual. We list BLEU-5 scores of our monolingual model in Table 1. Compared with the NMT baseline implemented under transformer architecture with the same setting, our model get an average improvement of +0.947 BLEU over the state-of-art performance.

Table 1. Translation results (BLEU-5 score) for English-Chinese task in monolingual constraint.

System	NIST05	NIST06	NIST08	Ave
NMT baseline	24.227	24.72	17.67	22.613
Our model	$24.529^{+0.302}$	$24.91^{+0.19}$	$18.793^{+1.123}$	$23.560^{+0.947}$

Moreover, we find that our method achieves a substantial decrease of the number of <UNK>. As shown in Table 2, the <UNK> frequency drops by 30.84% in NIST05 and other test sets all enjoy a decrease to some extent. The reason behind is that relation modeling provides sufficient training for words which is hard to handle before. As shown in Table 4, "blew" is not familiar to original model which is represented as <UNK>. In our method, "blew" is the past form of "blow" and that relation (blew, blow, past-style of verb) is fully modeled to get better embedding representations.

Table 2. Statistics of the descent rate for UNK in monolingual constraint.

System	NIST05	NIST06	NIST08	Ave
Our model	30.84%	7.27%	23.15%	19.25%

Bilingual. When testing the effect of bilingual constraint, we only filter the specific sentences of NIST05, NIST06, NIST08, which cover at least one trained entity. As shown in Table 3, the enhanced model with bilingual constraint outperforms the baseline system by an average BLEU score of 0.675.

Table 3. Translation results (BLEU-5 score) for English-Chinese task in bilingual case for the subset of NIST 05, 06 and 08.

System	NIST05$'$	NIST06$'$	NIST08$'$	Ave$'$
NMT baseline	21.519	21.693	13.872	19.594
Our model	$22.464^{+0.945}$	$22.343^{+0.65}$	$14.105^{+0.233}$	$20.269^{+0.675}$

Table 4. Translation examples, where our method is more capable of obtaining accurate translations than baseline NMT in monolingual constrain.

Source	Palestinian suicide bomber blew up bus, 7 dead and 30 injured.
Reference	巴赶死队成员引爆巴士7人死30人伤。
Baseline	巴勒斯坦自杀炸弹杀手<UNK>公共汽车7死30伤。
Our Model	巴勒斯坦自杀炸弹杀手引爆公共汽车7人死亡30人受伤。
Source	Days of heavy snow in Europe left may dead and transportation disrupted.
Reference	欧洲连日大雪多人死亡交通中断。
Baseline	欧洲大雪<UNK>，许多人死亡，交通中断。
Our Model	欧洲大雪几天，许多人丧生，交通受阻。
Source	The verification department found quite a few fake college diplomas.
Reference	鉴定部门发现，大学生们的证书中也有不少是假货。
Baseline	<UNK>发现不少假大学文凭。
Our Model	核查部门发现了不少假大学文凭。

4.4 Results on Analogy Prediction Test

To further investigate whether the learned word embeddings actually encode the semantic relations imposed by KG, we implement analogy prediction test on the trained embeddings, which aims to predict the missing head or tail word for a relation fact triple (head, tail, r), mentioned in Mikolov et al. [10].

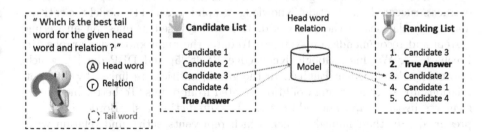

Fig. 5. An overview of analogy prediction task.

As illustrated in Fig. 5, given the head word and relation, our model has to select the proper tail word from five candidates by calculating the score as:

$$score(x) = |e_{head}M_r - e_x M_r + e_r| \tag{8}$$

We select 1K triples and swap their tail words. Our model ranks the candidates by their scores to evaluate the probabilities that being the true tail word. From the result shown in Table 5, the gold answers ranking the first account for 28.3% while the random baseline is 20%. It indicates that our model has some capacity of analogy prediction compared to randomly selection.

Table 5. The ranking results for gold answers in analogy prediction test.

Rank	1	2	3	4	5
Number	283	169	148	178	222

5   Related Work

Recently, neural machine translation has attracted more and more attention. A novel pure attention architecture, Transformer, is proposed by Vaswani et al. [15], which achieves state-of-art performance and has much faster training speed. Our model is also implemented under the Transformer framework.

Previous work mainly put emphasis on modeling the mapping function from source sentence to target sentence and external knowledge (e.g. knowledge graph) is in the absence of translate process. However, there are still some researches on how to enable knowledge to benefit translation. Li et al. [8] employed the "synonym" and "hypernym" relations extracted from Wordnet to find proper replacements for low-frequency words. Zou et al. [22] proposed that the embeddings of bilingual aligned words should be closer. Semantic gap between the source language string and its translation is minimized [19,20]. Synonyms extracted from dictionaries have been adopted to transform low-frequency word to adequate sequences [21]. Compared to their methods, we consider more diverse relation types between entities.

With respect to knowledge use in NMT, knowledge graph is a good choice to extract structured information. Knowledge graph is created to model the entities and their relations in the real world. It is widely used in question answering system and recommendation systems. To date, the main knowledge graphs are Freebase [3], Wordnet, Google Knowledge Vault [5] and DBPedia [1], which are mainly developed in English. In the graph, entities are linked by different relationships so that no one would be isolated from others. To better model the elements in the graph and address the link prediction task, Bordes et al. [4] presented a method named TransE which represents entity and relation with embedding and defines the arithmetic relations between the embeddings of head word, tail word and relation. Lin et al. [9] pointed out that entity and relation embeddings should be built in separate entity space and relation spaces. Besides, there existed many other model methods on entity and relation [11,14,16–18].

6   Conclusion

In this paper, we propose a method that integrates the external knowledge into NMT, aiming to augment the connections between the source words and their translations. We design two methods using entity relations as constraints to fully explore the usage of the knowledge graph in NMT. The first one is monolingual constraint which requires the embedding of the source words to hold the semantic relationship provided by KG. The second is bilingual constraint that enforces the semantic relation between the source words to be exactly maintained by their corresponding translations. Experimental results demonstrate that our method obtains much improvements over the strong NMT baseline.

Acknowledgements. The research work described in this paper has been supported by the National Key Research and Development Program of China under Grant No. 2016QY02D0303 and the Natural Science Foundation of China under Grant No. 61673380.

References

1. Auer, S., Bizer, C., Kobilarov, G., Lehmann, J., Cyganiak, R., Ives, Z.: DBpedia: a nucleus for a web of open data. In: Aberer, K., et al. (eds.) ASWC/ISWC -2007. LNCS, vol. 4825, pp. 722–735. Springer, Heidelberg (2007). https://doi.org/10.1007/978-3-540-76298-0_52
2. Bahdanau, D., Cho, K., Bengio, Y.: Neural machine translation by jointly learning to align and translate. In: International Conference on Learning Representations (2015)
3. Bollacker, K., Evans, C., Paritosh, P., Sturge, T., Taylor, J.: Freebase: a collaboratively created graph database for structuring human knowledge. In: SIGMOD Conference, pp. 1247–1250 (2008)
4. Bordes, A., Usunier, N., Garcia-Duran, A., Weston, J., Yakhnenko, O.: Translating embeddings for modeling multi-relational data. In: International Conference on Neural Information Processing Systems, pp. 2787–2795 (2013)
5. Dong, X., et al.: Knowledge vault: a web-scale approach to probabilistic knowledge fusion. In: ACM SIGKDD International Conference on Knowledge Discovery and Data Mining, pp. 601–610 (2014)
6. Dyer, C., Chahuneau, V., Smith, N.A.: A simple, fast, and effective reparameterization of IBM Model 2. In: Proceedings of the NAACL (2013)
7. Gehring, J., Auli, M., Grangier, D., Yarats, D., Dauphin, Y.N.: Convolutional sequence to sequence learning. arXiv:1705.03122 (2017)
8. Li, S., Xu, J., Miao, G., Zhang, Y., Chen, Y.: A semantic concept based unknown words processing method in neural machine translation. In: Huang, X., Jiang, J., Zhao, D., Feng, Y., Hong, Y. (eds.) NLPCC 2017. LNCS (LNAI), vol. 10619, pp. 233–242. Springer, Cham (2018). https://doi.org/10.1007/978-3-319-73618-1_20
9. Lin, Y., Liu, Z., Sun, M., Liu, Y., Zhu, X.: Learning entity and relation embeddings for knowledge graph completion. In: Twenty-Ninth AAAI Conference on Artificial Intelligence, pp. 2181–2187 (2015)
10. Mikolov, T., Yih, W.T., Zweig, G.: Linguistic regularities in continuous space word representations. In: HLT-NAACL (2013)
11. Nickel, M., Rosasco, L., Poggio, T.: Holographic embeddings of knowledge graphs. In: National Conference on Artificial Intelligence, pp. 1955–1961 (2016)
12. Papineni, K.: Roukos, S., Ward, T., Zhu, W.J.: BLEU: a method for automatic evaluation of machine translation. In: Meeting of the Association for Computational Linguistics, vol. 4, no. 4, pp. 307–318 (2001)
13. Sutskever, I., Vinyals, O., Le, Q.V.: Sequence to sequence learning with neural networks. In: International Conference on Neural Information Processing Systems, pp. 3104–3112 (2014)

14. Trouillon, T., Welbl, J., Riedel, S., Gaussier, E., Bouchard, G.: Complex embeddings for simple link prediction. In: International Conference on Machine Learning, pp. 2071–2080 (2016)
15. Vaswani, A., et al.: Attention is all you need. arXiv:1706.03762v5 (2017)
16. Wang, Z., Zhang, J., Feng, J., Chen, Z.: Knowledge graph embedding by translating on hyperplanes. In: Twenty-Eighth AAAI Conference on Artificial Intelligence, pp. 1112–1119 (2014)
17. Xiao, H., Huang, M., Hao, Y., Zhu, X.: TransA: an adaptive approach for knowledge graph embedding. Computer Science (2015)
18. Xiao, H., Huang, M., Zhu, X.: TransG: a generative model for knowledge graph embedding. In: Meeting of the Association for Computational Linguistics, pp. 2316–2325 (2016)
19. Zhang, J., Liu, S., Li, M., Zhou, M., Zong, C.: Bilingually-constrained phrase embeddings for machine translation. In: Meeting of the Association for Computational Linguistics, vol. 1, pp. 111–121 (2014)
20. Zhang, J., Liu, S., Li, M., Zhou, M., Zong, C.: Mind the gap: machine translation by minimizing the semantic gap in embedding space. In: National Conference on Artificial Intelligence, pp. 1657–1663 (2014)
21. Zhang, J., Zong, C.: Bridging neural machine translation and bilingual dictionaries. Computation and Language (2016)
22. Zou, W.Y., Socher, R., Cer, D.M., Manning, C.D.: Bilingual word embeddings for phrase-based machine translation. In: Empirical Methods in Natural Language Processing, pp. 1393–1398 (2013)

Improving Performance of NMT Using Semantic Concept of WordNet Synset

Fangxu Liu, JinAn Xu[✉], Gouyi Miao, Yufeng Chen,
and Yujie Zhang

School of Computer and Information Technology,
Beijing Jiaotong University, Beijing, China
{fangxuliu,jaxu,gymiao,chenyf,yjzhang}@bjtu.edu.cn

Abstract. Neural machine translation (NMT) has shown promising progress in recent years. However, for reducing the computational complexity, NMT typically needs to limit its vocabulary scale to a fixed or relatively acceptable size, which leads to the problem of rare word and out-of-vocabulary (OOV). In this paper, we present that the semantic concept information of word can help NMT learn better semantic representation of word and improve the translation accuracy. The key idea is to utilize the external semantic knowledge base WordNet to replace rare words and OOVs with their semantic concepts of WordNet synsets. More specifically, we propose two semantic similarity models to obtain the most similar concepts of rare words and OOVs. Experimental results on 4 translation tasks (We verify the effectiveness of our method on four translation tasks, including English-to- German, German-to-English, English-to-Chinese and Chinese-to-English.) show that our method outperforms the baseline RNNSearch by 2.38–2.88 BLEU points. Furthermore, the proposed hybrid method by combining BPE and our proposed method can also gain 0.39–0.97 BLEU points improvement over BPE. Experiments and analysis presented in this study also demonstrate that the proposed method can significantly improve translation quality of OOVs in NMT.

Keywords: NMT · Semantic concept of synset · Rare words · Unknown words

1 Introduction

In the past few years, Neural Machine Translation (NMT) has made rapid progress and it has shown state-of-the-art performance [1–3]. However, for the purpose of reducing the computational complexity, NMT typically needs to limit its vocabulary scale to an appropriate size, and this leads to rare word and OOV problems. Both Sutskever et al. [13] and Bahdanau et al. [1] observed that sentences with high ratio of rare words tend to be translated much more poor than sentences mainly containing frequent words.

To address the rare word and OOV problems, researchers have proposed several different methods. Luong et al. [4] proposed to annotate target unknown words with positional information to track their alignments. This method utilizes the position information, but it lacks the ability of taking advantage of linguistic knowledge such as syntax and semantics. Sennrich et al. [5] and Wu et al. [3] proposed to address the rare

© Springer Nature Singapore Pte Ltd. 2019
J. Chen and J. Zhang (Eds.): CWMT 2018, CCIS 954, pp. 39–51, 2019.
https://doi.org/10.1007/978-981-13-3083-4_4

word problem by splitting the words into sub-word units through unsupervised learning. These methods significantly alleviate the rare word problem and have been widely used in practice. However, these methods also suffer from the problem caused by the sparseness of rare words in the monolingual corpus used to train BPE or wordpiece model. Thus the rare word problem still remains challenging.

In this paper, to address the rare word problem, we propose to replace the rare words and unknown words with their semantic concepts of WordNet synsets so as to better obtain their semantic information during training and testing. Different from traditional methods, our method explicitly integrates the concepts embedding of rare words and unknown words into NMT, and it can better learn the semantic representations of rare words and unknown words. An example is shown in Fig. 1:

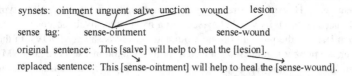

Fig. 1. An illustration of our main idea. We address rare words or OOVs of sentences in training set, and the rare words "ointment", "unction", "unguent" and "salve" are synonyms and they can be replaced and represented with their same semantic concept tag "sense-ointment". Also, rare words "wound" and "lesion" have the same treatment.

More specifically, during training, for the rare words in English side, we first collect their synonyms using WordNet [6], and annotate the rare words with the most similar semantic concepts. Then this new bilingual corpus with rare words replaced will be used to train a NMT model. To get the most similar semantic concepts of rare words, two models were proposed: (1) a RNN LM-based similarity model to compute the similarity on continuous space; (2) a statistical LM-based similarity model to compute the similarity on discrete space. During testing, we determine the detailed method according to the factor that English is the source or target language: (1) If English is the source language, we first replace the rare words with their semantic concept tags, and then the sentences are translated by the trained NMT model; (2) If English is the target language, the target sequence of words generated from the decoder of NMT may contain some semantic concept tags of rare words. We use attention mechanism and the bilingual phrase table to restore the semantic concept tags and get the final translation. Figure 2 illustrates the processing of our method.

Experiments show that our method can improve performance by up to 1.79 and 1.4 BLEU points over PosUnk [4] on the WMT 14 translation tasks of English-to-German and German-to-English, respectively. It can also outperform the PosUnk system by up to 1.32 and 1.03 BLEU points on English-to-Chinese and Chinese-to-English tasks, respectively. Furthermore, the proposed hybrid method by combining BPE and our method can also gain 0.39–0.97 BLEU points improvement over BPE.

Fig. 2. An example of processing rare words for training and testing

2 Neural Machine Translation and Impact of Rare Words

This section will briefly introduce the NMT method, and analyze the impact of the rare words on NMT

2.1 Neural Machine Translation

Attention-based encoder-decoder framework [1] is used in most of the state-of-the-art NMT models. The encoder consists of a bidirectional recurrent neural network (Bi-RNN), which reads a source sequence $X(x_1,\ldots,x_t)$ and generates a sequence of forward hidden states $\vec{h} = \left(\vec{h_1}, \vec{h_2}, \ldots, \vec{h_n}\right)$ and a sequence of backward hidden states $\overleftarrow{h} = \left(\overleftarrow{h_1}, \overleftarrow{h_2}, \ldots, \overleftarrow{h_n}\right)$. We obtain the annotation h_i of each source word x_i by concatenating the forward hidden state $\vec{h}$ and the backward hidden state $\overleftarrow{h}$; then they are calculated using two RNNs from left-to-right and right-to-left, respectively, as follows:

$$\vec{h}_i = f_{RNN}(x_i, \vec{h}_{i-1}). \tag{1}$$

$$\overleftarrow{h}_i = f_{RNN}(x_i, \overleftarrow{h}_{i-1}) \tag{2}$$

The decoder consists of a RNN, an attention network and a logical regression network. At each time step i, the probability $p(y_i|y_{<i}, \theta)$ is computed as follows:

$$p(y_i|y_{<i}, \theta) = g(s_i, y_{i-1}, c_i) \tag{3}$$

where the hidden state s_i is generated based on the previous hidden state s_{i-1}, the previous predicted word y_{i-1}, and the context vector c_i:

$$s_i = f_{RNN}(y_{i-1}, s_{i-1}, c_i) \tag{4}$$

where c_i is calculated as a weighted sum of the source annotations.

$$c_i = \sum_{k=1}^{n} \alpha_{jk} h_k \tag{5}$$

A detailed description can be found in Bahdanau et al. [1]

2.2 Impact of Rare Words

As discussed in the introduction part, the rare word problem has two major negative effects: first, treating all the unknown words as the same *unk* symbol undermines the semantic integrity of the sentences; second, the sparseness of rare words makes it difficult to learn better representation from training data.

To illustrate the impact of rare words to translation, we designed the following experiment: A thousand sentences were extracted from the United Nations parallel corpus English-to-Chinese translation data set. And then these sentences were translated by NMT model. Finally, we manually analyzed the translation accuracy of words with different frequencies. The results in Fig. 3 show that the words with higher frequency tend to be better translated, while the words with lower frequency typically tend to be incorrectly translated.

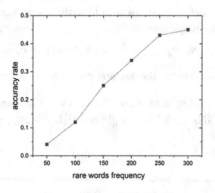

Fig. 3. Frequency vs. accuracy

3 Methodology

The analysis in the above section shows that the rare words have a considerable influence on the translation performance. So we propose to replace rare words in training and testing data with their semantic concepts by employing the semantic knowledge resource WordNet [6]. Specifically, we design two strategies of semantic similarity model to obtain the most similar semantic concepts of the rare words:

- RNN LM-based model, which computes the similarity on continuous space.
- Statistical LM-based model, which calculates the similarity on discrete space.

To illustrate our method, we introduce a parallel sentence pair as an example, as shown in Fig. 4(a). Note that the brackets indicate the rare word of the source side and its counterpart of the target side. From WordNet, we can get the semantic concepts of "ointment", as shown in Fig. 4(b). It shows how the semantic concepts of word "ointment" are organized in WorNet [6].

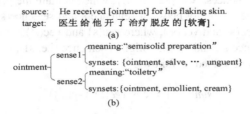

Fig. 4. An example of illustrating our method. (a) A parallel sentence pair. (b) The semantic concepts of "ointment" in WordNet.

3.1   WordNet

WordNet [6] is a large lexical database of English. Nouns, verbs, adjectives and adverbs are grouped into sets of cognitive synonyms (synsets), each expressing a distinct concept. Words in the same set of semantic concepts have the same meaning and typically can be used in the same context. These concepts are separately organized into four networks, and each semantic concept corresponds to a synonym set. The semantic concepts are connected by various relationships, such as synonymy, hypernym and hyponymy. In this paper, we leverage synonymy to process the rare words and OOVs.

3.2   Model 1: RNN LM-Based Similarity Model

Our first model seeks to employ sense embedding and neural language model to obtain the most similar semantic concepts of rare words

We illustrate our model 1 with a concrete example in Fig. 4. To get the most similar semantic concept of the rare word "ointment", we first collect all the synsets of the word "ointment" from WordNet, and each synset expresses a distinct semantic concept. In this case, the collected synsets are described: $synset_1 = \{$ ointment, ..., unguent $\}$ and $synset_2 = \{$ ointment, cream, emollient$\}$, and the two synsets correspond semantic concepts $sense_1$ and $sense_2$, respectively. Then we construct the semantic concept embeddings of the word "ointment" based on its synsets, namely $synset_1$ and $synset_2$. Specifically, the vector of $sense_1$ can be expressed as a weighted average of all embeddings of words in synset$_1$. Formally, the vector representation of semantic concept 'sense$_i$' is calculated as follows:

$$vec(sense_i) = \frac{vec('word_1') + \cdots + vec('word_n')}{n} \tag{6}$$

where word$_j$ ($1 \leq j \leq n$) denotes a word in synset$_i$, n is the number of words in synset$_i$, and the embedding of word$_j$ is learned from LSTM-RNN language model [7] that trained on large scale monolingual corpus.

As illustrated in Fig. 5, we determine the most similar semantic concept of the rare word "ointment". More specifically, word embedding of "ointment" in sentence s1 is replaced with sense$_1$ and sense$_2$ and thus two new sentences s2 and s3 are generated. We define a set of sentences, S = {s2, s3 ...}, which contain the generated sentences. Then we compute the similarity between sentence s and sentence s' by means of the cosine distance of vec(s) and vec(s'), where vec(s) and vec(s') are the embeddings of sentence s and sentence s', and s is the original sentence (i.e. s1), s' is from set S. The similarity formula is described as follows:

$$sim(s, s') = \cos(vec(s), vec(s')) \tag{7}$$

where we use the last hidden state (i.e. h_t in Fig. 5) as the sentence vector.

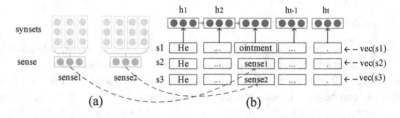

Fig. 5. An example of selecting the most similar semantic concept

Finally, the semantic concept, which embedded in the sentence s' with the highest similarity, is chosen as the most similar semantic concept w_{sense}, as follows:

$$s_{W_{sense}} = \arg\max_{s' \in S} sim(s, s') \tag{8}$$

After obtaining the most similar semantic concept of a rare word, we replace the rare word with its most similar semantic concept and get a sentence with the semantic concept tag (i.e. "He received [sense$_1$] for his flaking skin.", where sense$_1$ is the semantic concept calculated by formula 8.).

3.3   Model 2: Statistical LM-Based Similarity Model

Similar to Model 1, our Model 2 first collect all the synsets of the word "ointment" from WordNet (i.e. synset$_1$ and synset$_2$ in Sect. 3.2), and each synset denote a distinct semantic concept. Unlike Model 1, we seek to determine the most similar semantic concept of the rare word "ointment" by computing the score of semantic concepts. Specifically, for each synset, we construct a list of sentences, which is described as $S = \{s_1, s_2, \ldots, s_n\}$, by replacing the rare word with each word of the synset. Then we compute the score of the semantic concept with the following equation:

$$\text{score}(sense_i) = \frac{lm(s_1) + lm(s_2) + \ldots + lm(s_n)}{n} \tag{9}$$

where n is the number of sentences in S, $lm(s_i)$ is the statistical language model (3-g) score of the sentence s_i $(1 \leq i \leq n)$, and the statistical language model is trained on large scale monolingual corpus.

Finally, we choose the semantic concept with the highest score as the most similar semantic concept

$$w_{sense} = \underset{1 \leq i \leq n}{\arg \max} \, score(sense_i) \tag{10}$$

3.4   Integrating Semantic Concepts into NMT

In this section, we seek to explicitly integrate semantic concepts in NMT by replacing rare words with their corresponding semantic concept tags. We describe our work in detail in training and testing phases. Note that, we only handle the words with frequency less than M in the training data and in the scope of WordNet [6]. And the effects of different threshold M is compared in Sect. 4.2.

During training, for each sentence pair of the parallel corpus, we replace the rare words in the English side with the most similar semantic concept tags by applying model 1 or model 2. And then the new generated parallel corpus is fed into NMT for training. We also need to learn word level alignment for sentence pairs in the bilingual corpus. As a byproduct, a lexical translation table can be derived from the aligned bilingual corpus. Our method can also combine with BPE: first we replace the rare words with the most similar semantic concept tags, and the remaining rare words will be split into sub-word units by BPE.

During testing, if English is the source language, the rare words in the source sentence will be first replaced with their corresponding semantic concept tags, and then the new sentence will be translated by the trained NMT model. If a target word e_j in the translation aligns to a semantic concept tag of the source side, we will restore e_j to the translation of the original source word via the lexical translation table and attention mechanism, where the lexical translation table is derived from the aligned bilingual corpus and it provides word level alignment for sentence pairs, and the attention mechanism provides a kind of soft alignment that helps to find the corresponding source word for each target word. In another case, if English is the target language, first the trained NMT model will translate the test sentence and get the translation that may contains concept tags. Then we track the source words of the concept tags by attention mechanism. With the help of the lexical translation table and the language models (3-g), the concept tags will be restored to the translation of the source words and get the final translation result.

4 Experiments

We evaluate the effectiveness of the proposed method on English-to-German, German-to-English, English-to-Chinese and Chinese-to-English translation tasks. Translation quality is measured by the BLEU metric [8].

4.1 Experimental Settings

We performed experiments with attention-based RNNSearch [1] system on corpus extracted from the shared translation task of WMT 2014[1] (German ↔ English) and the United Nations parallel corpus v1.0 [9] (Chinese ↔ English). For German ↔ English translation, the training set contained about 3.5 million sentence pairs. For Chinese ↔ English, the training set contained about 3 million sentence pairs. Further, we used GIZA++ to obtain the alignment information from the same bilingual data. We trained a neural language model on monolingual data that contained about 10 million English sentences extracted from the WMT 2014. In addition, the statistical language model was trained with SRILM [10]. We used WMT newstest2013 as our development set, and reported results on newstest2012 and newstest2014 for German ↔ English. Besides, we used the open development set and the test set provided in the UN parallel corpus for Chinese ↔ English.

The hyperparameters were set as follows: the number of the hidden units was 512 for both the encoder and decoder, and the word embedding dimension was 512 for all source and target words. The parameters in the network were updated with the adadelta algorithm, a minibatch size of 64, and reshuffled the training set between epochs. We used a beam size of 10 for the beam search, with probabilities normalized by the sentence length. The dropout method was used at the readout layer, and the dropout rate was set to 0.5.

4.2 Preliminary Experiments

A preliminary experiment was performed to determine the threshold M and the vocabulary size V mentioned in Sect. 3.4. We experimented on English-to-German translation task and chose WMT newstest2013 as the test set. We set different threshold M and vocabulary size V during the experiment, and recorded the number of unknown words. The experimental results are shown in Tables 1 and 2:

---

[1] http://www.statmt.org/wmt14.

Table 1. Unknown words of different M and V in newstest2013

V	M				
	Baseline	250	200	100	50
30000	2363	2203	2259	2281	2309
40000	1920	1714	1742	1783	1861
50000	1661	1521	1546	1604	1627

Table 2. BLEU scores (%) of different M and V

V	M				
	Baseline	250	200	100	50
30000	16.52	**17.26**	17.03	16.80	16.61
40000	17.69	18.37	**18.46**	18.12	17.87
50000	18.91	19.48	**19.52**	19.28	19.20

As seen from Table 1, when the threshold M is 250 and the vocabulary size V is 50000, newstest2013 contains fewer unknown words. Similarly, the results in Table 2 show that, when M is 200, we can gain a better BLEU score.

Based on the results of Tables 1 and 2, for reducing the computational complexity, the threshold M is set to 200 and the vocabulary size is set to 40000 in our comparative experiments.

4.3 Comparative Experiments and Main Results

There are 8 different systems in our comparative experiments

1. RNNSearch: Our baseline NMT system with improved attention mechanism.
2. PosUnk: The system, proposed by Luong et al. [4], annotated target *unk* as *unk-k*, where k indicates the position information of the source word.
3. w2v&lm&restore: The system, proposed by Li et al. [11], replaced the unknown words with the similar in-vocabulary words.
4. wn&lm&restore: The system, proposed by Li et al. [12], replaced the unknown words of source language (English) with the similar in-vocabulary words using WordNet.
5. ours-model1&restore: Our system, presented in Sect. 3.2, replaced rare words and unknown words with their semantic concept tags using our model1.
6. ours-model2&restore: Our system, presented in Sect. 3.3, replaced rare words and unknown words with their semantic concept tags using our model2.
7. BPE: The system, proposed by Sennrich et.al [5], decorated rare words with sub-word units.
8. ours-model1&BPE: We first address rare words using the proposed ours-model1&restore, and the remaining rare words are processed by BPE.

The remaining unknown words in system 3–system 6 (w2v&lm&restore, wn&lm&restore, ours-model1&restore, ours-model2&restore) were processed by the method of PosUnk. We use the same dataset and network parameters to train the comparison model, as seen in Sect. 4.1.

On English-to-German translation task, as seen in Table 3, our method outperforms the RNNSearch by 2.88 BLEU points and surpasses the other three traditional methods (PosUnk, w2v&lm&restore, wn&lm&restore) by 0.46–1.79 BLEU points. And the results show that ours-model1& BPE (our method combined with BPE) can achieve 0.49 BLEU points improvement over BPE. Also, the results in Table 4 show that ours-model1&restore and ours-model1& BPE can achieve improvement on English-to-Chinese translation task. Generally, our approach can effectively improve translation performance by processing rare words of the source side.

Table 3. English → German BLEU scores (%) of different systems

System	13(dev)	12	14	Average
RNNSearch	17.69	15.22	15.55	16.15
PosUnk	18.80	16.23	16.69	17.24
w2v&lm&restore	19.87	17.35	17.68	18.30
wn&lm&restore	20.02	17.73	17.98	18.57
ours-model2&restore	**19.92**	**18.01**	**18.13**	**18.68**
ours-model1&restore	**20.25**	**18.39**	**18.45**	**19.03**
BPE	21.37	19.33	19.29	19.99
ours-model1&BPE	**21.98**	**19.82**	**19.66**	**20.48**

Table 4. English → Chinese BLEU scores (%) of different systems.

System	UN(dev)	UN(test)	Average
RNNSearch	34.03	34.60	34.31
PosUnk	35.41	35.95	35.68
w2v&lm&restore	36.49	36.63	36.56
wn&lm&restore	36.83	36.74	36.78
ours-model2&restore	**36.97**	**36.89**	**36.93**
ours-model1&restore	**37.05**	**36.96**	**37.00**
BPE	37.93	37.89	37.91
ours-model1& BPE	**38.34**	**38.27**	**38.30**

On German-to-English translation task, the results in Table 5 show that our method outperforms the baseline RNNSearch by 2.55 BLEU points. It also surpasses the systems PosUnk and w2v&lm&restore by 1.4 and 0.65 BLEU points, respectively. And the results show that ours-model1&BPE (our method combined with BPE) can gain 0.74 BLEU points improvement over BPE. In addition, the results in Table 6 show that ours-model1&restore and ours-model1&BPE can also achieve improvement on Chinese-to-English translation task. In general, our approach can effectively improve translation performance by processing rare words of the target side.

Table 5. German → English BLEU scores (%) of different systems

System	13(dev)	12	14	Average
RNNSearch	22.51	19.64	20.04	20.73
PosUnk	23.69	20.86	21.11	21.88
w2v&lm&restore	24.58	21.21	22.10	22.63
ours-model2&restore	**24.60**	**21.42**	**21.93**	**22.65**
ours-model1&restore	**25.26**	**21.98**	**22.62**	**23.28**
BPE	26.23	23.89	25.15	25.09
ours-model1&BPE	**26.92**	**24.47**	**26.11**	**25.83**

Table 6. Chinese → English BLEU scores (%) of different systems.

System	UN(dev)	UN(test)	Average
RNNSearch	41.33	41.86	41.60
PosUnk	42.58	43.32	42.95
ours-model2&restore	43.04	43.96	43.50
w2v&lm&restore	43.10	44.06	43.58
ours-model1&restore	**43.55**	**44.41**	**43.98**
BPE	43.80	44.75	44.28
ours-model1& BPE	**45.01**	**45.50**	**45.25**

4.4   Analysis

Analysis of Translation Performance

From the results in Sect. 4.3, our proposed method can achieve significant improvement and outperform the traditional methods [4, 11, 12]. Different from previous work, we replace rare words and unknown words with similar semantic concepts, and explicitly integrate semantic concepts into NMT. Thus, the concept embeddings of rare words and unknown words are used when training neural networks, which enhance the ability of NMT models to learn better semantic representation of rare words and unknown words.

Currently, BPE is an effective method which splits the rare words into sub-word units. However, fine-grained sub-word units lead to a certain degree of loss of semantic information. Unlike BPE, our work focuses on enhancing NMT model by obtaining accurate semantic information of rare words. Intuitively, our method and BPE are complementary to each other. The results in Sect. 4.3 shows that the hybrid method by integrating BPE and our proposed method can achieve significant improvement on all translation tasks.

Analysis of *unk* Translation

To have a further insight into the translation quality of our method, we manually analyzed the effect of the translation of *unk* in English-to-Chinese and Chinese-to-English translation tasks. The results are shown in Table 7:

Table 7. Translation accuracy of unknown words, where the test set provided in the UN parallel corpus, contains 4000 sentences. "*": indicates that the number of *unk* to be processed and it is equal to the number of *unk* appearing in RNNSearch. "-": indicates that the method cannot process unknown words of Chinese.

System	English-to-Chinese		Chinese-to-English	
	Total(unk)	Correct	Total(unk)	Correct
RNNSearch	941	103(11%)	1179	230(19%)
PosUnk	*	205(22%)	*	336(28%)
w2v&lm&restore	*	272(29%)	*	379(32%)
wn&lm&restore	*	285(30%)	-	-
ours-model1&restore	*	320(34%)	*	414(35%)
BPE	*	375(39%)	*	506(42%)
ours-model1&BPE	*	417(44%)	*	554(46%)

From the data in Table 7, on English-to-Chinese and Chinese-to-English translation tasks, one observes that in general more unknown words can be correctly translated in our improved system than in the baseline system. Accordingly, replacing unknown words with their semantic concepts can better maintain the integrity of the sentences and effectively improve the translation accuracy of the unknown words.

Analysis of the Applicability Scope of Our Method

Since our approach resorts to the external semantic knowledge resources (i.e. WordNet [6]), our study is suited to translation tasks that contain languages supported by semantic knowledge resources. More importantly, our research is a further attempt to integrate semantic knowledge into NMT and the experimental results demonstrate that the proposed method can effectively improve the translation accuracy.

5 Conclusion

Rare words problem is a major factor that affect the performance of NMT. To address this problem, we propose to use the external semantic knowledge base WordNet to replace rare words and unknown words with their semantic concepts of WordNet synsets, and explicitly integrate the concept embeddings of rare words into NMT, which can help NMT model better capture the semantic information of rare words. Experiments on 4 translation tasks show that the proposed method can significantly improve the translation quality. Further analysis shows that our method is able (1) to better capture the word sense of rare words, (2) to improve the translation accuracy of unknown words, (3) to combine BPE and achieve a certain improvement over BPE.

In future work, we will explore further strategies to integrate semantic concepts into NMT. Additionally, we also hope to explore a general way to solve the problem that the acquisition of semantic information is limited by semantic resources (i.e. WordNet [6]).

Acknowledgments. The research work has been supported by the National Nature Science Foundation of China (Contract 61370130, 61473294 and 61502149), and Beijing Natural Science Foundation under Grant No. 4172047, and the Fundamental Research Funds for the Central Universities (2015JBM033), and the International Science and Technology Cooperation Program of China under grant No. 2014DFA11350.

References

1. Bahdanau, D., Cho, K., Bengio, Y.: Neural machine translation by jointly learning to align and translate. In: ICLR 2015 (2015)
2. Vaswani, A., et al.: Attention is all you need. CoRR abs/1706.03762 (2017)
3. Wu, Y., Schuster, M., Chen, Z., et al.: Google's neural machine translation system: bridging the gap between human and machine translation (2016)
4. Luong, M.T., Sutskever, I., Le, Q.V., et al.: Addressing the rare word problem in neural machine translation. Bull. Univ. Agric. Sci. Vet. Med. Cluj-Napoca. Vet. Med. **27**(2), 82–86 (2014)
5. Sennrich, R., Haddow, B., Birch, A.: Neural machine translation of rare words with subword units. Computer Science (2015)
6. Miller, G.A.: WordNet: a lexical database for English. Commun. ACM **38**(11), 39–41 (1995)
7. Palangi, H., Palangi, H., Deng, L., Shen, Y.: Deep sentence embedding using long short-term memory networks: analysis and application to information retrieval. IEEE/ACM Trans. Audio Speech Lang. Process. **24**(4), 694–707 (2015)
8. Papineni, K., Roukos, S., et al.: BLEU: a method for automatic valuation of machine translation. In: Proceedings of 40th Annual Meeting of the Association for Computational Linguistics, Philadelphia, Pennsylvania, USA, July 2002, pp. 311–318 (2002)
9. Ziemski, M., Junczys-Dowmunt, M., Pouliquen, B.: The United Nations Parallel Corpus, Language Resources and Evaluation (LREC 2016), Portorož, Slovenia, May 2016 (2016)
10. Stolcke, A.: SRILM—an extensible language modeling toolkit. In: International Conference on Spoken Language Processing, pp. 901–904 (2002)
11. Li, X., Zhang, J., Zong, C.: Towards zero unknown word in neural machine translation. In: International Joint Conference on Artificial Intelligence, pp. 2852–2858. AAAI Press (2016)
12. Li, S., Xu, J., Miao, G., Zhang, Y., Chen, Y.: A semantic concept based unknown words processing method in neural machine translation. In: Huang, X., Jiang, J., Zhao, D., Feng, Y., Hong, Yu. (eds.) NLPCC 2017. LNCS (LNAI), vol. 10619, pp. 233–242. Springer, Cham (2018). https://doi.org/10.1007/978-3-319-73618-1_20
13. Sutskever, I., et al.: Sequence to sequence learning with neural networks. In: Advances in Neural Information Processing Systems, pp. 3104–3112 (2014)

Cross-Lingual Semantic Textual Similarity Modeling Using Neural Networks

Xia Li[1,2(✉)], Minping Chen[2], and Zihang Zeng[2]

[1] Key Laboratory of Language Engineering and Computing,
Guangdong University of Foreign Studies, Guangzhou, China
[2] School of Information Science and Technology/School of Cyber Security,
Guangdong University of Foreign Studies, Guangzhou, China
shelly_lx@126.com, minpingchen@126.com,
raymondtseng0912@126.com

Abstract. Cross-lingual semantic textual similarity is to measure the semantic similarity of sentences in different languages. Previous work pay more attention on leveraging traditional NLP features (e.g., alignment features, syntactic features) to evaluate the semantic similarity of sentences. In this paper, we only use word embedding as basic features without any handcrafted features and build a model which is able to capture local and global semantic information of the sentences to evaluate semantic textual similarity. We test our model on SemEval-2017 and STS benchmark datasets. Our experiments show that our model improves the performance of the semantic textual similarity and achieves the best results compared with the baseline neural-network based methods reported on the two datasets.

Keywords: Cross-lingual semantic textual similarity · SemEval-2017
Neural networks

1 Introduction

Cross-lingual semantic textual similarity measures the degree to which two sentences in different languages are semantically equivalent to each other, which is a fundamental language understanding problem in many fields, such as information retrieval, information extraction, machine translation and so on. Evaluation of sentence semantic similarity in English has achieved great success, but there are still some challenges in modeling sentences similarity in different languages due to lacking of enough training data for a particular language [1, 2]. In this paper, we focus on building a model to evaluate the semantic similarity between cross-lingual sentence pairs. We translated all the foreign languages into English by Google translator[1] following the state-of-the-art works in SemVal-2017 [3–5].

---

[1] https://cloud.google.com/translate/.

© Springer Nature Singapore Pte Ltd. 2019
J. Chen and J. Zhang (Eds.): CWMT 2018, CCIS 954, pp. 52–62, 2019.
https://doi.org/10.1007/978-981-13-3083-4_5

Most previous works focus on leveraging traditional NLP features to evaluate the semantic similarity between cross-lingual sentence pairs [3, 4]. These hand-crafted features helped improve the performance of the models, but also are expensive for the system.

Few work only used neural features without any hand-crafted features in modeling semantic textual similarity between cross-lingual sentence pairs. Shao et al. [5] is one of the few exceptions. They use convolutional neural network to capture the semantic representation of the source and target sentences, and then fed both of them into the fully connected layer to get the semantic similarity scores of the two sentences. The model achieved good results in the task of SemVal-2017.

However, the model only captured the local semantic information of a sentence by CNN. The local n-grams information captured by CNN sometimes doesn't work well when modeling the semantic textual similarity in cross-lingual sentences. This is because when a language is translated into another language[2], the words order of the translated sentence may change or be inaccurate due to translation errors. Therefore, obtaining local n-grams information of a sentence through CNN may be insufficient due to the wrong words order caused by the translation.

On the other hand, in the task of cross-language semantic textual similarity, we not only need to pay attention to the local semantic matching information between sentences, but also need to consider the global semantic information of the sentences. Therefore, in order to better measure the semantic similarity of two sentences, we should integrate the semantic information of the source and target sentences in both local and global aspects as much as possible.

Based on these observations, this paper proposes a model which is able to capture the local and global semantic information between cross-lingual sentence pairs. Firstly, we use CNN with kernels of multiple sizes to capture the local matching information between sentence pairs. Then, we use the recurrent neural network to capture the semantic dependences of the sentence words and use this accumulation of the semantic relationship as the global semantic information of the sentence and output an accumulated vector of the sentence. Finally, the local information and the global information are concatenated to represent the final semantic of the sentence.

The architecture of our model is showed as Fig. 1. We do several experiments on SemVal-2017 data and STS benchmark data and the experimental results show that our model outperforms the current best neural network model without any manual NLP features.

2 Model

2.1 Sentence Encoding

Each source sentence and target sentence are initially represented by a fixed-size word-embeddings matrix. We use padding operation in our model. Supposing the maximum length of the sentence in our model is L, then if the number of words in a sentence is

---

[2] In this paper, all the other languages are translated into English.

less than L, we will add 0 to it. If the number of words in a sentence exceeds L, we will remove the extra words. All the words in the sentence are converted into corresponding word embedding, and then we can get a matrix representation of the sentence. Source sentence matrix and target sentence matrix are inputted into the model as sentence initial encoding.

2.2   Local Semantic Information Extraction

In order to capture the local matching information of the sentence pair sufficiently, we use convolution blocks of different convolution kernel sizes to convolve the sentences. As shown in Fig. 1, we convolve the sentences using three convolution blocks with convolution kernel windows of 1, 2, and 3, each with 300 convolution kernels. We also use ReLu function as activation function in CNN layer and maximum down-sampling for extracting the most informative vector from the output of convolution. The outputs of the three convolutional blocks pooling are jointed as a 900-dimensional semantic vector which represents the local semantic information of the sentences.

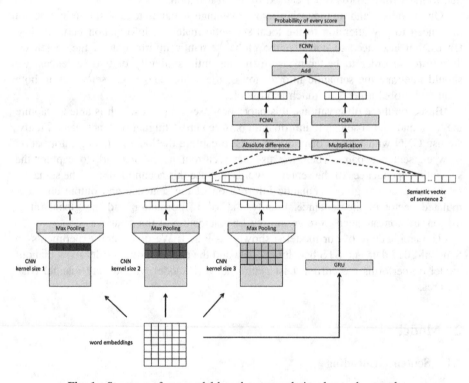

Fig. 1. Structure of our model based on convolutional neural network.

2.3   Global Semantic Information Extraction

In the cross-lingual sentence semantic similarity evaluation task, although the word order of the translated sentence may change, the semantic information of most words is correct.

Therefore, our motivation is to capture the global semantic information of the sentence through the information accumulation operation of the recurrent neural network.

Different from the previous work, our model does not take the average of the output of each GRU [6, 7] unit as the final output, but accumulates the semantic information of each word from left to right and takes the output of the last GRU unit as the final representation of the global semantics of the sentence (Fig. 2). Assuming that a sentence consists of m words $S = \{w_1, w_2, ..., w_m\}$. We use GRU to produce the internal states for the sequence at each timestep t: $(y_1, y_2,..., y_{m-1}, ..., y_m)$. As for our task, we use the last hidden state output y_m as the result of RNN with GRU units. We believe that this output accumulates the global semantic information of the sentence. As the output of GRU is also a 300-dimensional semantic vector, we concatenate the 900-dimensional local semantic vector obtained in Sect. 2.2 and the 300-dimensional global semantic vector as a 1200-dimensional vector and take it as a final semantic representation of the comprehensive information of the sentence.

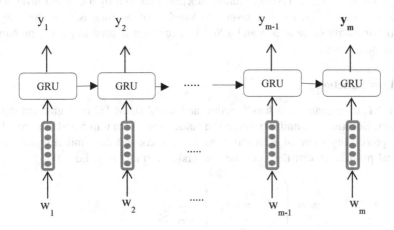

Fig. 2. Global semantic information extraction from GRU.

2.4 Representation of Semantic Similarity of Sentence Pairs

In order to calculate the text semantic similarity of two sentences, following Shao et al. [5], we carry two kinds of operations to the semantic representations of two sentences: absolute difference and multiplication. Here, the absolute difference operation for two sentences can be considered as getting the difference information between two semantic vectors, and the multiplication operation for two sentences can be considered as capturing the similarity information of two semantic vectors.

Different from the work of Shao et al. [5], we do not directly concatenate these two vectors of absolute difference operation and multiplication operation to get a final vector to represent the semantic similarity of sentence pairs. Instead, we firstly input the difference result vector and the multiplication result vector to a fully connected layer respectively. Then we add the two output vectors from these two fully connected layers and take it as a final representation of semantic similarity of the source sentence and target sentence. The formula is shown in Eqs. (1)–(3).

$$h\_sub = W_1 \times \left| \overrightarrow{SV_1} - \overrightarrow{SV_2} \right| + b_1 \tag{1}$$

$$h\_mul = W_2 \times \left| \overrightarrow{SV_1} \cdot \overrightarrow{SV_2} \right| + b_2 \tag{2}$$

$$\overrightarrow{SDV} = h\_sub + h\_mul \tag{3}$$

Here $\overrightarrow{SV_1}$ and $\overrightarrow{SV_2}$ are the final semantic vectors of the two sentences. W_1, b_1, W_2, b_2 are weights used in fully connected layers. The number of neurons used here is 900. $\overrightarrow{SDV}$ is the final representation of semantic similarity between two sentences. We put $\overrightarrow{SDV}$ into a fully connected layer and the Softmax layer. The fully connected layer has 900 neurons and use the Tanh activation function followed by a dropout layer with a dropout rate of 0.5. At the last layer, the number of neurons is 6 as the range of semantic similarity score is 0–5 and a Softmax function is used to get the probability value of each score.

2.5   Loss Function

We use KL divergence as a loss function and use ADAM [8] as a gradient descent optimizer. Because the similarity score is a value range from 0 to 5 and our model will get the probability value of each score, we need to convert the similarity score into a fractional probability distribution. The conversion formula is as Eq. (4).

$$p_i = \begin{cases} y - |y|, & i = |y| + 1 \\ |y| - y + 1, & i = |y| \\ 0, & otherwise \end{cases} , i \in [0, K] \tag{4}$$

Where K is the maximum similarity score. Loss function is the KL divergence between the standard fractional probability distribution p and the predicted fractional probability distribution $\hat{p}_\theta$. KL divergence can effectively measure the difference between two distributions and when two distributions are the same, the value is zero. The loss function of our model is shown in Eq. (5).

$$J(\theta) = \frac{1}{m} \sum_{k=1}^{m} KL(p^{(k)} || \hat{p}_\theta^{(k)}) + \frac{\lambda}{2} \|\theta\|_2^2 \tag{5}$$

Here m is the total number of sentence pairs in the training set, k represents the kth sentence pair in the training set, θ_2^2 is the L2 loss of parameters in the network, λ is coefficient of L2 loss.

3 Experiments

3.1 Datasets

In our experiment, we use two datasets as our training data and test data. Because of the need for large size of training data, following work of [3–5], we collect the English sentence similarity dataset in the text semantic similarity task from SemEval-2012 to SemEval-2016 as our training data[3]. We randomly divide the collected data into 10 parts. 90% of the data is used as training data which contains 13,191 sentence pairs in total, and the other 10% of the data is used as a development set which contains 1,465 sentence pairs. We use multi-lingual and cross-lingual dataset [2] in the text semantic similarity task in SemEval-2017 as our test data[4]. In this task [2], there are 7 tracks with total 1750 sentence pairs, each track has 250 sentence pairs. The details of the SemEval-2017 data are shown in Table 1.

Table 1. Details of SemEval-2017 dataset.

Track	Language	Test pairs
1	Arabic (ar-ar)	250
2	Arabic-English (ar-en)	250
3	Spanish (es-es)	250
4a	Spanish-English (es-en)	250
4b	Spanish-English (es-en)	250
5	English (en-en)	250
6	Turkish – English (tr-en)	250
Total	–	1750

We also use the SST benchmark dataset in SemEval-2017[5] to test our model. The training data in SST benchmark contains 5749 sentence pairs, the development set contains 1500 sentence pairs, and the test set contains 1379 sentence pairs. Details of the two datasets are shown in Table 2.

Table 2. Details of two datasets used in our experiments.

Task	Training data	Test data	Development data
SemEval2017 Task1	13191	1465	1750
STS benchmark	5749	1500	1379

---

[3] http://ixa2.si.ehu.es/stswiki/index.php/Main_Page.

[4] http://alt.qcri.org/semeval2017/task1/index.php?id=data-and-tools.

[5] http://ixa2.si.ehu.es/stswiki/index.php/STSbenchmark.

3.2   Experimental Setup

We use the Pearson correlation coefficient as our evaluation metric in our experiment following SemEval-2017 task. The Pearson correlation coefficient can be used to reflect the degree of linear correlation between the two variables in a range of $[-1, 1]$. In our experiment, the Pearson correlation coefficient is calculated between the gold similarity score graded by human and the predicted similarity score graded by our model.

We implement some preprocessing operations for the data which include: (1) Remove all punctuations in the sentences; (2) Transform all words into lowercase; (3) Use NLTK segmentation to segment words; (4) Use pretrained paragram[6] word embedding [9] to represent the words of sentences. If the word does not exist in the paragram vocabulary, it is set to 0. (5) The length of all sentences is converted to a fixed size of 30. Those sentences with size larger than 30 will be cut, and shorter than 30 will be filled in zero. The hyperparameters used in our experiments are shown in Table 3. The initial leaning rate of our model is set to 0.001 and the batch size is 64. Besides, a dropout rate of 0.5 and regularization of 0.004 are used to avoid overfitting.

Table 3. Parameters of our model

Steps	Paramters	Value
Preprocessing	Sentence size	30
	Dimension of paragram	300
Similarity computing model	Convolution kernel size	1,2,3
	Convolution kernels	300
	Convolution neural network activation function	Relu
	Fully connection layer neuros (first layer)	900
	Fully connection layer neuros (second layer)	6
Training	Optimizer	ADAM
	Minimum batch size	64
	Learning rate	0.001
	Dropout rate	0.5
	Regularization	0.004

3.3   Experimental Results and Analysis

We do several experiments on SemEval-2017 Task1 and STS benchmark datasets. In our experiments, we use top 3 systems on SemEval-2017 Task1 and top 4 systems on STS benchmark as our baselines [3–5, 9]. Among these four systems, the Rank 1 system (ECNU) [3] ensembled several machine learning methods and three neural network models with rich traditional NLP features. These features include a total of 67 manual features such as sentence pair matching features, n-gram overlaps features, sequence features, syntactic parse features, machine translated based features,

---

[6] https://drive.google.com/file/d/0B9w48e1rj-MOck1fRGxaZW1LU2M/view.

alignment features and single sentence features etc. The Rank 2 system (BIT) [4] was completely based on traditional features. The system introduced semantic information space (SIS), which is constructed based on the semantic hierarchical taxonomy in WordNet, to compute non-overlapping information content (IC) of sentences. The system ranks 2nd on SemEval-2017 Task1. And the Rank 3 system (HCTI) [5] was a neural-network based method which only used convolutional neural networks to capture the semantic information of the sentences without any handcrafted features.

Results on SemEval-2017. As shown in Table 4, the average Pearson correlation coefficient of our model in the SemEval-2017 Task1 dataset is 69.61 which is higher than the rank 2 system BIT model [4] for 1.72% and higher than the rank 3 system HCTI [5] for 3.64%. Compared with neural-network based system [5], our model outperforms on 6 tracks, especially on track 4b which is Spanish to English, our model outperforms for 9.55%. Although our model achieves better results than the neural-network based systems HCTI [5] and also outperforms than traditional-features based system BIT [4], the results of the work ECNU [3] are better than ours. As ECNU used 67 rich traditional NLP features and ensembled different machine learning methods and neural network models, it is more powerful to model the sentence pairs and can integrate the advantages of different models. However, compared with neural-network-based models, which can automatically learn the features of the sentences, the work to extract the features of ECNU is very heavy and time-expensive.

Table 4. Results of different methods on SemEval-2017 Task1 dataset.

Models	Primary	Track1 AR-AR	Track2 AR-EN	Track3 SP-SP	Track4a SP-EN	Track4b SP-EN-WMT	Track5 EN-EN	Track6 EN-TR
ECNU [3]	73.16	74.40	74.93	85.59	81.31	33.63	85.18	77.06
BIT [4]	67.89	74.17	69.65	84.99	78.28	11.07	84.00	73.05
HCTI [5]	65.98	71.30	68.36	82.63	76.21	14.83	81.13	67.41
Our model	69.61	74.37	72.96	81.13	80.22	24.38	83.34	70.90

Results on STS Benchmark Dataset. As shown in Table 5, on the STS benchmark dataset, the Pearson correlation coefficient on the development data is 85.41% and is 79.38% on test data. According to the STS benchmark Wiki, our model achieves the best performance on the dev data and the rank 3 on the test data. However, compared with neural-network-based models without any feature engineering, our model achieves the best results.

Table 5. Results of different methods on STS benchmark dataset.

	Dev	Test
ECNU [3]	84.70	81.00
BIT [4]	82.91	80.85
DT TEAM [18]	83.00	79.20
HCTI [5]	83.32	78.42
Our model	85.41	79.38

4 Related Work

In recent years, neural-network based methods have achieved excellent results in many different tasks. Some previous work has used neural network methods in the field of semantic text similarity [1–7, 9–13]. The word embedding [14, 15] generated by the neural network is a basic research work for calculating the similarity of texts for neural-network based methods. Word embedding is low-dimensional real number vector unsupervised trained from large-scale texts, aiming to represent tokens. This representation can better reflect the contextual semantics of the word. It can better solve the problem brought by traditional bag of the words such as high-dimensional sparseness and lack of sequences semantics. Some widely used word embeddings are Word2Vec [16] and Glove [17].

Many studies used word embeddings as the basis features to calculate text similarities through various formulas or models. Kusner et al. [18] thought that the minimum movement distance needed to move all the words from one text to the corresponding word in the word vector space is the similarity of the two texts. This method only considered the semantics of words ignoring the semantics of the entire sentence or the entire document which can cause deviations when computing similarities. Pagliardini et al. [19] proposed a sen2vec model based on the word vector. They used n-grams to combine the word vectors into sentence vectors and extended the word context to the sentence context. The experimental results showed that sentence vectors can express semantic information more effectively. Tai et al. [20] used the long short-term memory network (LSTM) [21] and bidirectional long short-term memory network (BiLSTM) to calculate semantic text similarity. At the same time, the syntactic analysis was introduced in the long short-term memory network which further mined the semantic information through the semantic dependency tree. Although this method can effectively extract the global semantic information of sentences, it is computationally intensive and does not work well for the long texts, and it did not pay attention to local information in sentences which is important for sentence textual similarity.

Different from previous works which used many traditional NLP handcrafted features to evaluate the semantic similarity of sentences [3, 4], Shao et al. [5] used a convolutional neural network to calculate the similarity of semantic texts, but their model only used a convolution kernel of size 1 which only can focus on the local information of the unigram without considering global information of sentences.

In this paper, we build a text similarity calculation model based on the convolutional neural network without any traditional NLP features. Also, different from previous methods, we represent the sentences with the local and global semantic information. We use convolution kernels of size 1, 2 and 3 to capture unigrams, bigrams and trigrams information as local information vectors of the sentence and use the last hidden output of recurrent neural network with GRU units to capture the global semantic information of the sentence. Combining vectors with local and global information into one vector which can be regarded as a final semantic representation of the sentences. We perform absolute difference and multiplication operations on the source and target sentence and then input them into a fully connected layer respectively, and we can get a final representation of the semantic similarity of the sentence pair by adding operation. Several experiments showed that our model performs well on SemEval-2017 task1 and STS benchmark datasets.

5 Conclusion

In this paper, we build a model to evaluate cross-lingual sentence semantic textual similarity based on the neural networks without any traditional manual NLP features. Different from previous models, we represent the sentence pairs with joint of the local and global semantic information captured from the sentence. We use three kinds convolution kernels of window size 1, 2 and 3 to capture unigrams, bigrams and trigrams information as local semantic information vectors of the sentence. And then, we use recurrent neural network with GRU units and take the last hidden states as the global semantic information of the sentence. We combine these vectors with local and global semantic information into a vector to be a final representation of the semantic of the sentences. In order to get the semantic similarity of the sentences, we perform absolute difference and multiplication operations on the sentence pair and then input them into a fully connected layer respectively, getting a final representation of the semantic similarity of the sentence pair. We test our model on SemEval-2017 Task1 and STS benchmark datasets. Despite the simplicity of our model, the results of our several experiments in two datasets show that our model has a good performance.

There is still some work to do with our model in the future. First, the words order of a sentence may change when it is translated from one language into English, but the relationship between each two words anywhere in the sentence is relatively constant. Therefore, in the future, we will consider incorporating the self-semantic relationship of the words of a translated sentence into the semantic representation of the sentence in order to improve the performance of the model. In addition, we also see that the ECNU system [3] still outperforms our neural network system due to the use of rich traditional features. In the future, we will consider incorporating traditional features into neural network to enhance learning and improve the performance of the model.

Acknowledgement. This work is supported by the National Science Foundation of China (61402119) and Special Funds for the Cultivation of Guangdong College Students' Scientific and Technological Innovation. ("Climbing Program" Special Funds.)

References

1. Agirre, E., et al.: Semeval-2016 Task 1: semantic textual similarity, monolingual and cross-lingual evaluation. In: Proceedings of the 10th International Workshop on Semantic Evaluation (SemEval-2016), pp. 497–511 (2016)
2. Cer, D., Diab, M., Agirre, E., Lopez-Gazpio, I., Specia, L.: SemEval-2017 Task 1: semantic textual similarity-multilingual and cross-lingual focused evaluation. arXiv preprint arXiv: 1708.00055 (2017)

3. Tian, J., Zhou, Z., Lan, M., Wu, Y.: ECNU at SemEval-2017 Task 1: leverage kernel-based traditional nlp features and neural networks to build a universal model for multilingual and cross-lingual semantic textual similarity. In: Proceedings of the 11th International Workshop on Semantic Evaluation (SemEval-2017), pp. 191–197 (2017)

4. Wu, H., Huang, H.Y., Jian, P., et al.: BIT at SemEval-2017 Task 1: using semantic information space to evaluate semantic textual similarity. In: Proceedings of the 11th International Workshop on Semantic Evaluation (SemEval-2017), pp. 77–84 (2017)

5. Shao, Y.: HCTI at SemEval-2017 Task 1: use convolutional neural network to evaluate semantic textual similarity. In: Proceedings of the 11th International Workshop on Semantic Evaluation (SemEval-2017), pp. 130–133 (2017)

6. Cho, K., Van Merriënboer, B., Bahdanau, D., Bengio, Y.: On the properties of neural machine translation: encoder-decoder approaches. arXiv preprint arXiv:1409.1259 (2014)

7. Chung, J., Gulcehre, C., Cho, K., Bengio, Y.: Empirical evaluation of gated recurrent neural networks on sequence modeling. arXiv preprint arXiv:1412.3555 (2014)

8. Kingma, D.P., Ba, J.: Adam: a method for stochastic optimization. CoRR abs/1412.6980 (2014)

9. Wieting, J., Bansal, M., Gimpel, K., Livescu, K.: Towards universal paraphrastic sentence embeddings. arXiv preprint arXiv:1511.08198 (2015)

10. Agirre, E., Diab, M., Cer, D., Gonzalez-Agirre, A.: Semeval-2012 Task 6: a pilot on semantic textual similarity. In: Proceedings of the First Joint Conference on Lexical and Computational Semantics-Volume 1: Proceedings of the Main Conference and the Shared Task, and Volume 2: Proceedings of the Sixth International Workshop on Semantic Evaluation, pp. 385–393 (2012)

11. Agirre, E., Cer, D., Diab, M., Gonzalez-Agirre, A., Guo, W.: * SEM 2013 shared task: semantic textual similarity. In: Second Joint Conference on Lexical and Computational Semantics (* SEM), Volume 1: Proceedings of the Main Conference and the Shared Task: Semantic Textual Similarity, vol. 1, pp. 32–43 (2013)

12. Agirre, E., et al.: Semeval-2014 Task 10: multilingual semantic textual similarity. In: Proceedings of the 8th International Workshop on Semantic Evaluation (SemEval 2014), pp. 81–91 (2014)

13. Agirre, E., et al.: Semeval-2015 Task 2: semantic textual similarity, English, Spanish and pilot on interpretability. In: Proceedings of the 9th International Workshop on Semantic Evaluation (SemEval 2015), pp. 252–263 (2015)

14. Hinton, G.E.: Learning distributed representations of concepts. In: Proceedings of the Eighth Annual Conference of the Cognitive Science Society, vol. 1, p. 12, (1986)

15. Bengio, Y., Ducharme, R., Vincent, P., Jauvin, C.: A neural probabilistic language model. J. Mach. Learn. Res. 3(6), 1137–1155 (2003)

16. Mikolov, T., Sutskever, I., Chen, K., Corrado, G. S., Dean, J.: Distributed representations of words and phrases and their compositionality. In: Advances in Neural Information Processing Systems, pp. 3111–3119 (2013)

17. Pennington, J., Socher, R., Manning, C.: Glove: global vectors for word representation. In: Proceedings of the 2014 Conference on Empirical Methods in Natural Language Processing (EMNLP), pp. 1532–1543 (2014)

18. Kusner, M., Sun, Y., Kolkin, N., Weinberger, K.: From word embeddings to document distances. In: International Conference on Machine Learning, pp. 957–966 (2015)

19. Pagliardini, M., Gupta, P., Jaggi, M.: Unsupervised learning of sentence embeddings using compositional n-gram features. arXiv preprint arXiv:1703.02507 (2017)

20. Tai, K.S., Socher, R., Manning, C.D.: Improved semantic representations from tree-structured long short-term memory networks. arXiv preprint arXiv:1503.00075 (2015)

21. Hochreiter, S., Schmidhuber, J.: Long short-term memory. Neural Comput. 9(8), 1735–1780 (1997)

The Impact of Named Entity Translation for Neural Machine Translation

Jinghui Yan[1](✉), Jiajun Zhang[2,3], JinAn Xu[1], and Chengqing Zong[2,3,4]

[1] Beijing Jiaotong University, Beijing, China
{17112083,jaxu}@bjtu.edu.cn
[2] National Laboratory of Pattern Recognition,
Institute of Automation, CAS, Beijing, China
[3] University of Chinese Academy of Sciences, Beijing, China
[4] CAS Center for Excellence in Brain Science
and Intelligence Technology, Beijing, China
{jjzhang,cqzong}@nlpr.ia.ac.cn

Abstract. Named entity translation has been shown in many studies that could have positive impact on performance of sentence level neural machine translation. In this paper, we study a mainstream structure that incorporating an external named entity translation model to neural machine translation. We give several comparison experiments by applying different named entity translation model structures, to clearly represent the impact of this structure in improving quality of neural machine translation. The experiments show that the proposed approach is able to achieve posistive result on some datasets and we give our analysis of influence factors.

Keywords: Named entity · Neural machine translation
Named entity translation

1 Introduction

Neural machine translation (NMT) achieved impressive result in recent years. Thanks to a series creative proposals of [1,5,6], such as "sequence-to-sequence" and "attention mechanism", there is a notable improvement in aspects of sentence accuracy and fluency. However, existence of out-of-vocabulary (OOV) is still a problem that neural machine translation always suffers from. For reducing computation complexity, the number of vocabulary of NMT system has to restricted to a limited size, due to which lots of rare words have to be replaced by *unk* symbols. Named entity, always playing as low-frequency words, is the main cause of OOV problem.

Many studies have been proposed to handle this problem. Zhang et al. [3] feed the pseudo-parallel sentences synthesized by an additional bilingual dictionary into the training of NMT in order to translate low-frequency words or phrases. One iconic work is [7], which presents a subword-level neural machine translation

© Springer Nature Singapore Pte Ltd. 2019
J. Chen and J. Zhang (Eds.): CWMT 2018, CCIS 954, pp. 63–73, 2019.
https://doi.org/10.1007/978-981-13-3083-4_6

model based on the byte pair encoding (BPE) algorithm [8]. BPE is a compression algorithm that originally developed for word segmentation, it can restrict vocabulary into a fixed size by segment word to subword, for instance, a rare named entity "Estelle" would be transfer into 'Estelle'. Though BPE could really transfer a rare word to a sequence of frequent subwords and generate a subword vocab file for a training corpus, there are still enormous amount of NE that we can not capture. Wang et al. [9] discusses the advantages and disadvantages of different translation granularities in Chinese-English NMT, but it does not lays emphasis on which granularity is the most suitable for named entity. Especially for transliteration words of named entities, there are innumerable combinations of subwords that a finite training set could never be covered totally.

To tackle the problems above, we propose to translate the named entities prior to the translation of whole sentence by an external named entity translation model. Li et al. [10] followed the "tag-replace" training method proposed by Loung et al. [11], using character level sequence to sequence model to translate named entities and an NMT model is trained on the new data of which named entities have been replaced with their type tags. In this paper, we propose to use different named entity translation models and a more general named entity alignment method to test the feasibility of this scheme. To verify the effectiveness of the scheme, we manually force all of named entities be exactly translated and the result will be present in Sect. 4.

2   Related Work

The research of named entity translation has come a long way. Earlier researchers focus on constructing a grapheme mapping table from source named entity A to a corresponding character of target B. Wan et al. [12] made mainly two mapping steps to translate English country names into Chinese names: English phoneme to Chinese pinyin, and Chinese pinyin to han characters. Some researchers try to use statistical methods to directly learn syllable alignment probabilities from bilingual named entity corpus. Li et al. [13] transliterated person names from English to Chinese used modified source-channel model for direct orthographic mapping to generated probabilistic rules from a bilingual dictionary. Ekbal et al. [14] using modified source-channel model that incorporates different linguistic knowledge of possible conjuncts for Bengali and English. Yang et al. [15] presented a two-step CRF model for machine transliteration. Recently, deep learning achieve impressive results for sentence level machine translation, inspired by which, researchers began to use neural machine translation model to automatically catch the features for NE translation. Cambria et al. [4] use statistical machine translation techniques to translate some existing English common knowledge content into Chinese. Li et al. [10] split both Chinese and English words into character level, using a "sequence-to-sequence" structure for named entity translation. Li et al. [16] segment the English words into subword level, building a subwords-to-characters model for English-Chinese person name transliteration and get an impressive result.

For the study of incorporating named entity translation into neural machine translation system, the mainstream approach is making NEs translation as a separating procedure from the original NMT model. Li et al. [10] trained a sentence level NMT model with NEs in parallel sentences tagged by NE symbols, then the NE symbols in output sentences will be replaced with corresponding translations, which is generated by its eternal NE translation module. Wang et al. [17] proposed similar method to Li [10] but only focus on PER named entities and only use the extracted parallel person names from training data. Their result brings no significant improvement but they claim it will be useful for human evaluation.

3   System Scheme

To verify the impact of named entity translating on neural machine translation, we propose to separate the NMT translating processing into two parts: named entity translating and other parts of sentences translating. The overview of our architecture shows in Fig. 3.

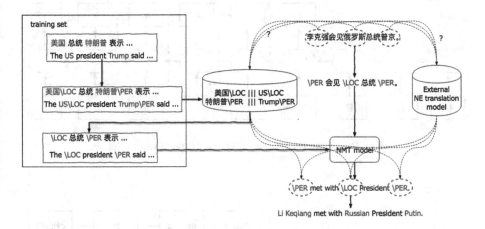

Fig. 1. System architecture of incorporating NE translation into neural MT

Tag Replacing. Prior to the training process of NMT, a word aligner together with NE recognizer are used to replace the named entities which parallelly appear in the training corpus with special tags as follows:

- "LOC1 总统 PER1表示..."
- "The LOC1 president PER1 said ..."

We use two monolingual NE recognizer on both sides of training set to recognize all NE inside corpus. Considering a named entity may contain multi-gram tokens, we need recombine them into unigrams. For instance, using underline to recombine "青沙公路" and "Tsing Sha Highway" to "青沙 _ 公路/LOC" and "Tsing_Sha_Highway/LOC" respectively. Then, a word alignment tool can be used to align and extract those pairs with same NE tags.

As shown in Fig. 3, a bilingual parallel NE dictionary can be generated by above steps, which is used to replace the NE appearing in parallel sentences pairs with tags.

External NE Translation. In order to adapt named entity translation to sequence-to-sequence (seq2seq) translation model, we need cut the word into more granular patterns. Here we build two kind of Chinese-English named entity seq2seq translation models. The first one is a character-to-character model which we split both Chinese and English parts into sequence of characters. For another one, we use BPE algorithm to segment named entities in English side into sequence of subwords. Then a character-to-subword NE translation model can be built. Figures 1 and 2 show the architectures of our two models respectively.

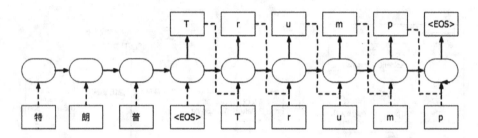

Fig. 2. Character-to-character NE translation model

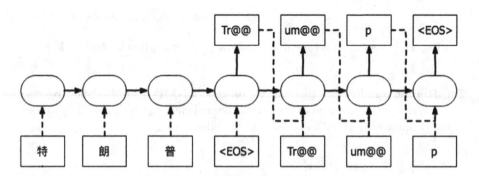

Fig. 3. Character-to-subword NE translation model

4 Experiment

4.1 Data Set

We use CWMT Chinese-English parallel data to train our NMT model, which contains about 9M sentences pairs. We choose NIST03 dataset as development and NIST 04-06 are used as test set. Meanwhile, LDC Chinese-English NE translation corpus [20] (LDC2005T34) which is compiled from Xinhua News Agency newswire texts, is used for building our named entity translation model. The entire LDC2005T34 corpus contains several categories of NEs (e.g., person, location, organization, press, industry). In our experiment, we only focus on person name, location and organization. After extracting these three categories of NEs, we split the train, dev, test set by their proportions Table 1 shows the statistics.

Table 1. Statistics of the data for building external NE translation model

Category	Number of entries			
	Total	Train	Dev	Test
PER	693,705	692,265	720	720
LOC	230,844	230,364	240	240
ORG	37,409	37,329	40	40
Total	961,958	959,958	1,000	1,000

4.2 Training Detials

We limit both the baseline NMT system and the tagged NMT system with vocabulary size of 30k Chinese subwords and 35k English subwords. We use Transformer [18] implementation of a self-attention based sequence-to-sequence NMT model. The batch size is 4096, and drop-out probability is 0.3. We use Adam gradient optimization [21] with learning rate 0.1. We stop training at 200k steps for both models when accuracy of tunning sets are not improved for both models. For our named entity translation system, we use same model structure with baseline NMT model. We split all Chinese named entities into characters. In character-to-character NE translation system, we split English named entities into characters too, except that we use '@' to replace the original blank inside those entities. For character-to-subword NE translation system, English NE are segmented into subwords by using BPE model, and we set the size of subword into 35k.

4.3 Performance and Results

NE Translation System. We totally build five NE translation models to test their performance in translating different kinds of named entities. As shown in

Table 1, we use total training data to built the character-to-character model (c2c-Total) and character-to-subword model. Also, we train three character-to-character models (c2c-PER, c2c-LOC, c2c-ORG) using each of the three categories individually to verify if a clearly classified named entity training model could be helpful. We only use accuracy to evaluate the result. Table 2 shows the evaluation result.

Table 2. Performance of different NE translation model

	PER	LOC	ORG
c2c-Total	37.5%	29.8%	29.2%
c2sub-Total	34.2%	27.3%	19.5%
c2c-PER	37.5%	-	-
c2c-LOC	-	28.2%	-
c2c-ORG	-	-	19.5%

Due to the multi-transliteration problem, all of five models give a poor performance of accuracy, lower than 40%. Compared vertically, character-to-character model performs a little bit better than character-to-subword model. We believe it is because that the subword segmentation can not completely include all combinations of English character sequences. In other words, the vocabulary of target side is still limited. Also, we can see that, building the model by category individually will not help performance much, but somehow drop a bit. We think there are two reasons here:

First, the NE data of different categories always nest inside each other. For example, the "Harvard University" is an organization named entity, however, part of the phrase "Harvard" could also be nested inside the person named entity "John Harvard" which would provide helpful translation information when translating "Harvard University". Second, there are lots of transliteration words in all kind of categories of named entities. For instance, the LOC named entity "Cassandra" and the PER named entity "Sandra" are share a common transliteration part "sandra". Therefore, it may be an unwise choice to individually build translation model by the category.

By horizontally comparing, it could be found that translation Performance of PER named entity always performs better than others. Chen [19] make analyses for Chinese-English named entity corpus LDC 2005T34, and she found that the transliterated entities take up 100% of PER, transliterated location names account for 89.4% of all LOC, and transliterated organization names take only 12.6% of ORG named entities. According to Chen's statistics, we surmise that better performance of PER entities are mainly due to a high rate of transliteration words, of which rules are easier to be learned.

More specifically, we check the named entities that are erroneously translated by tag-replace system. Table 3 shows some false examples. The first raw gives a typical example of wrong PER translating—the wrong domain. Obviously it is possible to translate 布希 into "Bouchy" if only considering the pronunciation, however, in some areas like Taiwan, people use 布希 a set of phrases to refer to president Bush. Raw 2 and raw 3 show another unavoidable problem—the NE translation model can not cover all rules of combinations of named entities, especially for the non-transliteration named entities. Because of the absent of combination "中国-China" or "南韩-south korean" inside the ex-NE dict, the NE translation model transliteration it character-for-character by using "中-naka; 国-kuni" and "南-nan; 韩-ham".

Table 3. Example of erroneously translated NE by tag-replace system

	NET	Baseline
布希	Bouchy	Bush
中国	Nakakuni	China
南韩	Nan ham	South korean

Named Entity Alignment. We use phrase-based SMT system Moses[1] to train named entity alignment. As the method mentioned in Sect. 3.1, we first recognize all named entities inside both source and target training sets, then we recombine them as a unigram token and put a tag followed. All aligned pairs are extracted from the phrase-table generated by Moses. We make a constraint of both source-target and target-source unigram phrase translating probability higher than 0.3. We totally extract 18,620 aligned pairs of named entities and Table 4 gives the statistic and its performance. Raw 3 and raw 4 are numbers of named entities recognised by Chinese and English monolingual named entity recognizer respectively.

Table 4. Performance of named entity alignment

	PER	LOC	ORG
Recognised (zh)	149,437	111,877	147,471
Recognised (en)	170,861	121,294	327,011
Extracted (pairs)	8,924	4,159	5,537
Accuracy	98%	94%	94%

To evaluate the alignment performance, we randomly select 100 extracted pairs of each NE category and analyse them manually. It could been seen from Table 4 that the alignment accuracy of all categories are pretty well. We also count the numbers of those extracted NE pairs tagged in the training sets.

---

[1] http://www.statmt.org/moses.

Sentence Translation Performance. According to the result in Sect. 4.3, we use only c2c-Total model in our external NE translation (ex-NET) system. The total Chinese-English named entity corpus LDC 2005T34 is used as our external named entity dictionary (ex-NE dict) and we use ex-NET system only when its corresponding translation can not be found in ex-NE dict. We train two NMT models, one of which we replace all three kinds of named entity (PER, LOC, ORG) inside training data with tags, the other of which we recongize PER named entities only. Table 5 shows the results of above two models in the second and third raw respectively.

Table 5. performance of NMT system (BLEU score)

	03 (dev)	04	05	06	Avg.
Baseline	40.33	40.53	40.43	39.66	40.23
tag-replace	35.33	37.98	37.91	35.67	36.72
tag-replace_PER_only	39.88	**41.53**	**40.61**	**40.83**	**40.71**
UNK	31.43	33.81	33.13	29.93	32.07

Table 6. Frequency of NE appeared in dev and test sets

	03	04	05	06
NE	1,874	2,983	2,219	1674
Lines	919	1,788	1,082	1,000
Words	23,534	49,151	29,355	23,917

Table 7. Comparison of NE translating performance in dev set.

	BLEU		Accuracy		
			PER	LOC	ORG
Baseline	40.33		32%	64%	47%
tag-replace	UNK	31.43	0%	0%	0%
	Oracle	40.58	100%	100%	100%
tag-replace_PER_only	UNK	36.71	0%	64%	47%
	Oracle	40.83	100%	64%	47%

Unfortunately, all test sets give depressing results to tag-replace system. However, in the third raw of the table, things are different. Except the development set, all other three test sets present improvements of BLEU score. For test sets 04 and 06, each of the increasing score are more than 1 BLEU scores, which can be seen as significant improvement.

More detaily, we count the frequency of NE appeared in each set in Table 6, which gives a intuitive feeling that there are numerosity named entities in test sets. To find the extent of the impact of the named entity translation for NMT, we build two control groups for both "tag-replace" and "tag-replace_PER_only" systems using development data set. We first replace all recognized named entities in translated output sentences with "UNK" tags, which means, for "tag-replace" system, all of three categories of named entities are not be translated. And for "tag-replace_PER_only" system, only PER named entities are not be translated and others keep the same translation accuracy with baseline system. The "UNK" group could be seen as the lower bound of the system. To find the upper bound of system, we manually replace all named entities with their correct translations, which we call the "Oracle" group. The result shows in Table 7—the accuracy of named entity translation of each group is calculated by comparing with the "Oracle" group. Comparing the two control groups, it prove that, named entity translation could deeply impact the quality of NMT. However, when comparing the "Oracle" group with the baseline, a notable phenomenon is that there is no expected improvement of "Oracle" group even we manually set 100% accuracy of named entity translation. Moreover, we keep the "Oracle" group of "tag-replace_PER_only" system the same accuracy of "LOC" and "ORG" with baseline and 100% accuracy of "PER", which perform better BLEU scores than the "Oracle" group of "tag-replace" system, though the latter has both higher accuracy of "LOC" and "ORG". Therefore, the unsatisfactory performance of "tag-replace" can not be merely attributed to the bad quality of external NE translation system

Sentences Translation. Prior to decoding procedure, same NE recognizer would be used to extract all named entities in input sentences and replace them with corresponding tags. Then, the system searches the NE dictionary generated by section 3.1 to find if there is given translations, otherwise the external NE translation model would be used to give the corresponding translations. As Fig. 3 shows, each of the tags in the NMT output will be directly replaced by its NE translating.

5   Conclusion

In this paper, we propose to verify the feasibility of separating the neural machine translation processing into two parts: named entity translation, and the other parts of sentences translating. The experiment proves that the quality of named entity translation will affect the final performance of whole sentences translating and the quality of named entity translation largely depend on if there are same domain knowledge between training set and the input named entities. The "tag-replace_PER_only" system in which we only recognize PER named entities inside sentences get a positive result of BLEU scores in neural machine translation However, the "tag-replace" system which handle all categories of named entities seems less effective in using named entity translation to improve quality of NMT system. Since the oracle system does not get a significant improvement, the unsatisfactory performance of "tag-replace" can not be merely attributed to the bad quality of external NE translation system. Moreover, we suspect that reordering could also be an influential factors of translation quality, due to the tags may damage the original sentence structures. We plan to incorporate a sentence type-based reordering model (Zhang et al. [2]) to handle the tags recording problem and find other influential factors in the future.

Acknowledgement. The research work described in this paper has been supported by the National Key Research and Development Program of China under Grant No. 2016QY02D0303 and the Natural Science Foundation of China under Grant No. 61673380.

References

1. Kalchbrenner, N., Blunsom, P.: Recurrent continuous translation models. In: Proceedings of the 2013 Conference on Empirical Methods in Natural Language Processing, pp. 1700–1709 (2013)
2. Zhang, J., Zong, C., Li, S.: Sentence type based reordering model for statistical machine translation. In: Proceedings of the 22nd International Conference on Computational Linguistics-Volume 1, pp. 1089–1096. Association for Computational Linguistics (2008)
3. Zhang J., Zong, C.: Bridging neural machine translation and bilingual dictionaries. arXiv preprint arXiv:1610.07272 (2016)
4. Cambria, E., Hussain, A., Durrani, T., Zhang, J.: Towards a Chinese common and common sense knowledge base for sentiment analysis. In: Jiang, H., Ding, W., Ali, M., Wu, X. (eds.) IEA/AIE 2012. LNCS (LNAI), vol. 7345, pp. 437–446. Springer, Heidelberg (2012). https://doi.org/10.1007/978-3-642-31087-4_46
5. Bahdanau, D., Cho, K., Bengio, Y.: Neural machine translation by jointly learning to align and translate. arXiv preprint arXiv:1409.0473 (2014)
6. Cho, K., et al.: Learning phrase representations using RNN encoder-decoder for statistical machine translation. arXiv preprint arXiv:1406.1078 (2014)
7. Sennrich, R., Haddow, B., Birch, A.: Neural machine translation of rare words with subword units. arXiv preprint arXiv:1508.07909 (2015)
8. Gage, P.: A new algorithm for data compression. C Users J. **12**(2), 23–38 (1994)
9. Wang, Y., Zhou, L., Zhang, J., Zong, C.: Word, subword or character? An empirical study of granularity in Chinese-English NMT. In: Wong, D.F., Xiong, D. (eds.) CWMT 2017. CCIS, vol. 787, pp. 30–42. Springer, Singapore (2017). https://doi.org/10.1007/978-981-10-7134-8_4
10. Li, X., Zhang, J., Zong, C.: Neural name translation improves neural machine translation. arXiv preprint arXiv:1607.01856 (2016)
11. Luong, M.T., Sutskever, I., Le, Q.V., Vinyals, O., Zaremba, W.: Addressing the rare word problem in neural machine translation. arXiv preprint arXiv:1410.8206 (2014)
12. Wan, S., Verspoor, C.M.: Automatic English-Chinese name transliteration for development of multilingual resources. In: Proceedings of the 17th International Conference on Computational Linguistics-Volume 2, pp. 1352–1356. Association for Computational Linguistics (1998)

13. Li, H., Zhang, M., Su, J.: A joint source-channel model for machine transliteration. In: Proceedings of the 42nd Annual Meeting on Association for Computational Linguistics, pp. 159–166. Association for Computational Linguistics (2004)
14. Ekbal, A., Naskar, S.K., Bandyopadhyay, S.: A modified joint source-channel model for transliteration. In: Proceedings of the COLING/ACL on Main Conference Poster Sessions, pp. 191–198. Association for Computational Linguistics (2006)
15. Yang, D., Dixon, P., Pan, Y.C., Oonishi, T., Nakamura, M., Furui, S.: Combining a two-step conditional random field model and a joint source channel model for machine transliteration. In: Proceedings of the 2009 Named Entities Workshop: Shared Task on Transliteration, pp. 72–75. Association for Computational Linguistics (2009)
16. Li, Z., Chng, E.S., Li, H.: Named entity transliteration with sequence-to-sequence neural network. In: 2017 International Conference on Proceedings of the Asian Language Processing (IALP), pp. 374–378. IEEE (2017)
17. Wang, Y., et al.: Sogou neural machine translation systems for WMT17. In: Proceedings of the Second Conference on Machine Translation, pp. 410–415 (2017)
18. Vaswani, A., et al.: Attention is all you need. In: Advances in Neural Information Processing Systems, pp. 5998–6008 (2017)
19. Chen, Y., Zong, C., Su, K., et al.: Joint Chinese-English named entity recognition and alignment. Chin. J. Comput. **34**(9), 1688–1696 (2011)
20. Huang, S.: LDC2005T34: Chinese <-> English named entity lists v 1.0. Linguistics Data Consortium (2005)
21. Kingma, D.P., Ba, J.: ADAM: a method for stochastic optimization. arXiv preprint arXiv:1412.6980 (2014)

Pivot Machine Translation Using Chinese as Pivot Language

Chao-Hong Liu[1]([⊠]), Catarina Cruz Silva[2], Longyue Wang[1], and Andy Way[1]

[1] ADAPT Centre, Dublin City University, Dublin, Ireland
ch.liu@acm.org, chaohong.liu@adaptcentre.ie
[2] Unbabel, Lisbon, Portugal

Abstract. Pivoting through a popular language with more parallel corpora available (e.g. English and Chinese) is a common approach to build machine translation (MT) systems for low-resource languages. For example, to build a Russian-to-Spanish MT system, we could build one system using the Russian–Spanish corpus directly. We could also build two systems, Russian-to-English and English-to-Spanish, as the resources of the two language pairs are much larger than the Russian–Spanish pair, and use them cascadingly to translate texts in Russian into Spanish by pivoting through English. There are, however, some confusing results on the Pivot MT approach in the literature. In this paper, we reviewed the performance of Pivot MT with the United Nations Parallel Corpus v1.0 (UN6Way) using both English and Chinese as pivot languages. We also report our system performance on the CWMT 2018 Pivot MT shared task, where Japanese patent sentences are translated into English using Chinese as the pivot language.

Keywords: Pivot MT · Pivot language · Patent MT

1 Introduction

The idea of Pivot MT is to build MT systems for a language pair where the availability of its parallel corpus (A–C) is either absent or comparably smaller than the existing parallel corpora paired with a 'pivot' language B, i.e. the A–B and B–C corpora [11,21]. When the availability of parallel corpus A–C is small, taking advantage of A–B and B–C corpora is the main approach to translating sentences from A to C. It is one of the enabling technologies to build MT systems for low-resource languages. There are many strategies in the literature on how to realise this idea in MT systems. Recently it was shown that zero-shot Neural Machine Translation (NMT) could also be trained in the same model for both A-to-C and C-to-A translation directions using only A–B and B–C corpora [6]. However, there is still a big gap on the results compared to the pivot approach of translating with cascading A-to-B and B-to-C models [12].

Two pivot strategies are compared in Utiyama and Isahara [21], namely phrase-translation and sentence-translation [21]. In the sentence-translation

© Springer Nature Singapore Pte Ltd. 2019
J. Chen and J. Zhang (Eds.): CWMT 2018, CCIS 954, pp. 74–85, 2019.
https://doi.org/10.1007/978-981-13-3083-4_7

strategy, the two models (FR-to-EN and EN-to-DE) were used directly. An input French sentence is first translated into an English sentence using the FR-to-EN model and then the MT-ed English sentence is translated into a German sentence using the EN-to-DE model. We refer to this sentence translation strategy as "Naïve Pivot MT" (or "Triangulation" in some literature). In the phrase-translation strategy, two Statistical MT (SMT) models are trained (FR-to-EN and EN-to-DE) and the phrase translation probabilities from the two phrase-tables are used to create a FR-to-DE phrase-table, which is then used along with a monolingual German language model (LM) in the FR-to-DE MT system.

In Wu and Wang [23], translation probabilities are interpolated using a small bilingual corpus. The method calculates phrase-translation probabilities and lexical weights from Source-to-Pivot and Pivot-to-Target MT models. The interpolated model for SMT [23] increased BLEU score by one point using 22,000 pairs of Chinese–Japanese parallel data [15].

The zero-shot translation approach, where only one neural network is trained with corpora of several translation pairs and directions, has also been proposed [6]. For example, in the training of that single neural network, Portuguese-to-English and English-to-Spanish directions are both used, with the idea that the one network is able to translate from Portuguese to Spanish, even though there is no direct Portuguese-to-Spanish parallel data used in training. However, in a later review of the approach, the scores using the UN6Way corpus [26] for Pivot MT are below 10 in terms of BLEU in most translation directions [12].

In this paper, we examine the idea of Pivot MT using the Naïve Pivot MT approach for comparison purposes. Both SMT and NMT approaches are employed as base models in the experiments. Our goal is to give an overview of the performance of Pivot MT in a fair setting and to clarify some confusing results reported in the literature, e.g. pivoting through English performed better than models trained with direct parallel corpora using the JRC-Acquis corpus [8,19].

The rest of the paper is organised as follows. In Sect. 2, we give an introduction to Pivot Machine Translation. In Sect. 3, our experiments are presented, followed by discussion in Sect. 4. Conclusions are given in Sect. 5.

2   Pivot Machine Translation

Pivot MT is the technology that we use to build A-to-C and/or C-to-A MT systems without (or with little) parallel data of the A–C language pair. A 'pivot' language B could be used to help build A–C MT systems if there are decent sizes of A–B and B–C parallel corpora to be taken advantage of [6,8,21,23].

In addition to the main Pivot MT approaches mentioned in Sect. 1, there are several strategies proposed to further improve pivoting performance. A joint training algorithm is introduced to connect the two separate models in the training phase [2]. Further work on the use of word embeddings in the pivot language is also suggested for Pivot NMT systems [6]. A method incorporating Markov random walks is introduced to alleviate the error propagation problem in Pivot MT, by connecting translation phrases of source and target languages [25].

A Teacher-Student Framework for zero resource NMT is proposed in [1]. The idea is to use a pivot-to-target NMT model (as "teacher") to guide the training of the source-to-target (the"student") model, in which source–target parallel data is not available. The framework might also work using SMT systems, but no experimentation exists on this.

An NMT-based pivot translation method has been proposed [5]. The architecture used in its 'one-to-one' strategy is the same as the "sentence translation strategy" described in [21]. The only difference is that SMT models are replaced by NMT models.

A single attention model is introduced to be shared across all language pairs, which enables the training of multi-way translation system in one NMT model [5]. Accordingly, the second strategy proposed in [5] is the use of 'many-to-one' translation in pivot MT. The strategy is while translating from ES to FR, the Spanish sentence is first translated into English using the ES-to-EN NMT model, and then from 'both' the original Spanish sentence and the MT-ed English sentence, into a French sentence using a "multi-way multilingual NMT" model. However, the two strategies do not perform well in the reports [5].

3   Experiments

We conduct our experiments on both SMT and NMT models. We used the case-insensitive 4-gram BLEU metric [15] for evaluation, and *sign-test* [3] for statistical significance testing.

We employ Moses [9] to build our phrase-based SMT models. The 5-gram language models are trained using the SRI Language Toolkit [20]. To obtain word alignment, we run GIZA++ [14] on the training data together with News-Commentary11 corpora. We use minimum error rate training [13] to optimize the feature weights. The maximum length of sentences is set as 80.

We employ an attentional encoder-decoder architecture as described in [16] using the Marian framework[1] [7], implemented in C++. We pre-process the data with similar routines in Moses[2] [9], using the following steps: entity replacement (applied to numbers, emails, urls and alphanumeric entities), tokenization, true-casing and byte-pair encoding (BPE) [17] with 89,500 merge operations. The models are trained on sentences of lengths up to 50 words with early stopping. Mini-batches were shuffled during processing with a mini-batch size of 80 sentences. The word-embedding dimension and the hidden layer size are 512. We selected the model that yields the best performance on the validation set.

For the experiments using the UN corpus, we built three MT systems (A-to-B, B-to-C and A-to-C) for each pivot triplet (A–B–C). The base MT model is either SMT or NMT. We used the default settings of Moses 4.0 as the base SMT model, and the Transformer model as implemented in [24] as the base NMT model.

---

[1] https://marian-nmt.github.io/.
[2] http://www.statmt.org/moses/.

There are more than ten million sentence pairs in the UN6Way corpus [4]. In addition to using the complete set of sentence pairs, we also randomly chose 500 K sentence pairs for the experiments. This random subset of UN6Way Corpus is referred to as UN6Way-500K in this paper in order to investigate the effect of increased training data size. The corpus contains the same sentences in each of the six languages, i.e. Arabic, Chinese, English, French, Russian and Spanish. However, we do not include experiments involving Arabic (in both SMT and NMT systems) and Russian (in SMT systems) as they require additional pre-processing and post-processing.

Chinese sentences are segmented using the open-source Jieba segmenter[3] [22]. Segmented Chinese sentences are used as source and target for the MT system training and test data. No additional pre-processing and post-processing tools are used. Likewise, tokenised English, French and Spanish following Moses 4.0 default settings are used as source and target for training and test data. Our experiments focus on comparing the MT performance with and without pivoting, i.e. A-to-C versus A-to-B-to-C using B as pivot.

3.1 Results of Direct MT Systems

The performance of SMT systems trained with the UN6Way-500K corpus is shown in Table 1. The results are obtained using direct (i.e. A-to-C) MT systems. We can see from the table that the BLEU scores of translations to and from Chinese are much lower than translations between any two of the three European languages (English, French and Spanish).

Looking at the scores of the two translation directions of one language pair in Table 1, it can be seen that inter-translations between two of the three languages, English, French and Spanish, are of the same MT performance in terms of BLEU scores. For example, EN-to-ES and ES-to-EN are 47.77 and 46.45, respectively. For translation pairs involving Chinese and Russian, however, the performance is quite different between the two translation directions of a language pair. For example, ZH-to-ES is 31.14 in terms of BLEU and ES-to-ZH is 18.91. There are more than 10 points difference in general between translations to and from Chinese.

Table 1. Evaluation of baseline Statistical Machine Translation (SMT) systems using 500 K pairs of UN6Way corpus to simulate a low-resource scenario

BLEU [%]	Target				
	EN	ZH	RU	ES	FR
EN		22.49	30.59	47.77	41.57
ZH	32.20		20.81	31.14	28.22
RU	40.23	19.38		39.32	35.24
ES	46.45	18.91	27.76		40.40
FR	41.80	17.80	26.66	43.75	

---

[3] https://github.com/fxsjy/jieba.

The performance of direct NMT systems trained with the UN6Way-500K corpus is shown in Table 2. We can also observe that scores of translations to and from Chinese are lower. However, NMT systems in general performed better than SMT systems to and from Chinese. Using the UN6Way-500K corpus for MT training, SMT performed better in some translation pairs and directions, e.g. FR-to-EN and ES-to-RU, and NMT performed better in others, e.g. ZH-to-EN and FR-to-ZH.

Table 2. Evaluation of baseline Neural Machine Translation (NMT) systems using 500 K pairs of UN6Way corpus to simulate a low-resource scenario

BLEU [%]	Target				
	EN	ZH	RU	ES	FR
EN		30.94	29.66	41.75	34.92
ZH	32.88		22.09	28.27	25.17
RU	36.82	25.22		31.70	28.40
ES	41.20	24.79	25.50		35.07
FR	37.12	23.10	23.51	37.16	

The results also show that despite UN6Way-500K being a relatively small corpus for NMT training, NMT models are able to outperform their SMT counterparts in most language pairs and translation directions involving Chinese. We believe this is because SMT relies on word segmenters to pre-process Chinese sentences, while NMT systems incorporate BPE to learn subword units during the training [17]. For other language pairs and translation directions, however, SMT outperformed NMT trained with small corpora.

The performance of SMT and NMT systems trained with the whole UN6Way corpus is shown in Tables 3 and 4, respectively. We can still observe that translations to and from Chinese are lower in general, but the differences between those language pairs not involving Chinese are smaller.

Table 3. Evaluation of base SMT systems using the complete UN6Way corpus (11M pairs)

BLEU [%]	Target				
	EN	ZH	RU	ES	FR
EN		37.87	43.29	61.22	50.07
ZH	42.88		29.61	39.65	34.49
RU	52.62	32.60		49.58	43.31
ES	59.83	31.25	39.72		49.70
FR	52.20	30.05	36.53	52.40	

Table 4. Evaluation of base NMT systems using the complete UN6Way corpus (11M pairs)

BLEU [%]	Target				
	EN	ZH	RU	ES	FR
EN		42.64	43.72	52.74	47.19
ZH	47.72		38.00	41.79	36.76
RU	48.39	35.46		41.67	38.23
ES	56.95	37.87	41.02		45.55
FR	48.28	34.03	36.58	46.13	

For direct SMT systems, when the size of the training corpus is increased from 500 K to 11M, the BLEU scores improve by 10 points in general. Systems translating into Chinese were observed to have a bigger improvement compared to other language pairs and translation directions, e.g. English-to-Chinese improves from 22.49 to 37.87 in terms of BLEU.

3.2 Results of Pivot MT Systems

In this section, the results of our Pivot MT systems are shown. They are derived from the same base systems in Tables 1 and 2. The scores of *-direct systems are repeated from either Tables 1, 2 or 4, for easier comparison with results using Pivot MT.

Table 5 shows the results of pivoting through English using SMT base systems trained with the UN6Way-500K corpus. It shows that for French and Spanish, direct MT in general outperformed pivoting through English by one to two points in terms of BLEU.

Table 5. Evaluation of SMT systems using EN as pivot language with the 500 K sample of data

BLEU [%]	Target			
	ZH	RU	ES	FR
ZH-en-pivot		19.81	30.68	27.52
RU-en-pivot	18.62		37.87	33.93
ES-en-pivot	19.30	27.23		38.47
FR-en-pivot	18.54	25.57	40.61	
ZH-direct		20.81	31.14	28.22
RU-direct	19.38		39.32	35.24
ES-direct	18.91	27.76		40.40
FR-direct	17.80	26.66	43.75	

Table 6 shows the results of pivoting through English using NMT base systems. It shows pretty much the same comparative results as those using SMT. For French and Spanish, the performance of pivoting through English is lower than direct NMT by two BLEU points. For translation directions involving Chinese, the performance is comparable. In general, comparing Tables 5 and 6, we see that performance with NMT is 2–5 BLEU points better than SMT. However, for some language pairs and translation directions (e.g. RU-to-ES), the SMT performance is much better (almost 8 BLEU points) than that of NMT. This is also observed in results using the complete set as training data. This experimental result will be examined further in future work.

Table 6. Evaluation of NMT systems using EN as pivot language with the 500 K sample of data

BLEU [%]	Target			
	ZH	RU	ES	FR
ZH-en-pivot		20.47	27.91	24.89
RU-en-pivot	23.70		31.49	28.15
ES-en-pivot	24.31	24.62		31.32
FR-en-pivot	23.11	22.96	33.29	
ZH-direct		22.09	28.27	25.17
RU-direct	25.22		31.70	28.40
ES-direct	24.79	25.50		35.07
FR-direct	23.10	23.51	37.16	

Table 7 shows the results of pivoting through English using NMT base systems where the whole UN6Ways corpus is used for training. The impact of using more data is significant. By increasing the training from 500 K to 11M, the BLEU scores have increased by 10 points in general for both direct models and pivot models

Table 7. Evaluation of NMT systems using EN as pivot language with the complete UN6Way corpus (11M pairs)

BLEU [%]	Target			
	ZH	RU	ES	FR
ZH-en-pivot		33.76	40.41	36.54
RU-en-pivot	35.06		41.74	38.14
ES-en-pivot	36.73	37.70		41.96
FR-en-pivot	33.46	34.48	42.77	
ZH-direct		38.00	41.79	36.76
RU-direct	35.46		41.67	36.76
ES-direct	37.87	41.02		45.55
FR-direct	34.03	36.58	46.13	

using English as pivot language. The gaps between results of direct models and pivot models are larger. This indicates that the pivot strategy is more suitable to be used in small corpus, and this is the situation we would like to employ it.

3.3   Impact of Pivot Choice

In addition to using English as pivot, we also conduct experiments using Chinese as the pivot language. Table 8 shows the results of pivoting through Chinese using SMT base systems trained with the UN6Way-500K corpus. One notable result is that the MT performance pivoting through Chinese to and from English, French and Spanish, is much lower than direct MT models by twelve BLEU points on average. The results are intuitive and confirm that it is beneficial to choose a pivot language that is linguistically close to both source and target languages.

Table 8. Evaluation of SMT systems using ZH as pivot language with 500 K sample

BLEU [%]	Target			
	EN	RU	ES	FR
EN-zh-pivot		23.94	34.64	30.87
RU-zh-pivot	29.06		29.49	26.72
ES-zh-pivot	31.50	21.48		29.34
FR-zh-pivot	29.83	21.05	31.12	
RU-en-pivot			37.87	33.93
ES-en-pivot		27.23		38.47
FR-en-pivot		25.57	40.61	

Table 9 shows the results of pivoting through Chinese using NMT base systems. It shows similar comparative results to those using SMT in Table 8. The gains replacing SMT base models with NMT ones are smaller (one to two points improvement in BLEU) compared to those using English as pivot language (four points improvement).

Table 9. Evaluation of NMT systems using ZH as pivot language with 500 K sample

BLEU [%]	Target			
	EN	RU	ES	FR
EN-zh-pivot		20.92	27.10	24.05
RU-zh-pivot	25.54		23.86	21.70
ES-zh-pivot	26.08	18.52		22.54
FR-zh-pivot	24.17	17.89	23.86	
RU-en-pivot			31.49	28.15
ES-en-pivot		24.62		31.32
FR-en-pivot		22.96	33.29	

3.4   Results of Japanese-to-English MT Using Chinese as Pivot Language

We participated in the CWMT 2018 shared task on Pivot MT. In this shared task, training corpora are given for the Japanese–Chinese and Chinese–English pairs in the patent domain. Participants trained the systems to translate from Japanese sentences into English using Chinese as the pivot language. We followed the same experimental setup as used for the UN6Way experiments, except pre-processing the segmentations on the Japanese and Chinese corpora. Common sequences of characters that appear in both Japanese and Chinese corpora are extracted (as parallel texts) from the training corpus and they are treated as 'words' by longest-word-first segmenters which were used to segment both Japanese and Chinese training corpora. The results of our system (designated as 'je-2018-S1-primary-a') is shown in Table 11. Our system took 4th place (out of 5) according to BLEU4-SBP score, but first place in terms of METEOR [10] and Translation Edit Rate (TER) [18].

Table 10. Evaluation of NMT systems using ZH as pivot language with the complete UN6Way corpus (11M pairs)

BLEU [%]	Target			
	EN	RU	ES	FR
EN-zh-pivot		34.60	40.66	35.83
RU-zh-pivot	39.21		36.42	32.84
ES-zh-pivot	40.37	31.73		34.44
FR-zh-pivot	36.51	29.62	36.10	
RU-en-pivot			41.74	38.14
ES-en-pivot		37.70		41.96
FR-en-pivot		34.48	42.77	

Table 11. Results of Pivot MT (Japanese-to-English) systems using Chinese as pivot language

Systems	BLEU4-SBP	NIST5	METEOR	TER
je-2018-S18-primary-a	0.4124	8.8276	0.3139	0.5297
je-2018-S20-primary-a	0.3904	8.6592	0.3075	0.5416
je-2018-S22-primary-a	0.3656	8.4550	0.2905	0.5636
je-2018-S1-primary-a	0.3428	8.2311	**0.3525**	**0.4811**
je-2018-S24-primary-a	0.3410	8.0863	0.3442	0.4926

4 Discussions

Our experiments using both SMT and NMT showed that pivoting will lose around 4 points compared to training with direct parallel data of comparable sizes. In [8], pivoting through English actually performed better than training MT in the direct language pair, in the JRC-Acquis corpus in the legal domain [19]. This finding is now not observed in our experiments using UN6Way.

For this result reported in [8], one possible cause might be that the corpus is curated 'aligned' around English, which might give pivoting through English an advantage compared to direct MT training on that particular corpus. Another reason might be that many texts in the JRC-Acquis corpus are in English in their original form [19]. Texts in the other languages are likely to be translations of their English counterparts. This would also give English an advantage when it is the pivot and explain why it performs better in pivot scenarios using the JRC-Acquis corpus.

5 Conclusions

In this paper we have reviewed major approaches to Pivot MT. Experiments using Naïve Pivot MT approaches were conducted to review the applicability of Pivot MT systems. Firstly, there were claims stating that pivoting through English outperformed direct trained MT systems. We found that using both the whole UN6Way Corpus and its random subset of 500 K sentences pairs, direct MT systems still outperform Pivot MT systems in general. Even when a very different language (i.e. Chinese to-or-from English, French and Spanish) is involved, their performance is still comparable. Secondly, the results showed in general that it would be much more beneficial to choose a pivot language that is linguistically close to the source and target languages. Thirdly, the results confirm that the errors introduced by pivoting do propagate to the target language. Therefore, it might be necessary to incorporate quality estimation and/or automatic/human post-editing to the intermediate translation of the pivot language, in application scenarios where high-quality translations are demanded.

Acknowledgements. The ADAPT Centre for Digital Content Technology is funded under the SFI Research Centres Programme (Grant No. 13/RC/2106) and is co-funded under the European Regional Development Fund. This work has partially received funding from the European Union's Horizon 2020 Research and Innovation programme under the Marie Skłodowska-Curie Actions (Grant No. 734211; the EU INTERACT project).

References

1. Chen, Y., Liu, Y., Cheng, Y., Li, V.O.: A teacher-student framework for zero-resource neural machine translation. In: Proceedings of the 55th Annual Meeting of the Association for Computational Linguistics (Volume 1: Long Papers), vol. 1, pp. 1925–1935 (2017)
2. Cheng, Y., Yang, Q., Liu, Y., Sun, M., Xu, W.: Joint training for pivot-based neural machine translation. In: Proceedings of the Twenty-Sixth International Joint Conference on Artificial Intelligence (IJCAI-17), Melbourne, Australia, pp. 3974–3980 (2017)
3. Collins, M., Koehn, P., Kucerova, I.: Clause restructuring for statistical machine translation. In: Proceedings of the 43rd Annual Meeting of the Association for Computational Linguistics, Ann Arbor, Michigan, USA, pp. 531–540 (2005)
4. Eisele, A., Chen, Y.: MultiUN: a multilingual corpus from united nation documents. In: Proceedings of the Seventh Conference on International Language Resources and Evaluation (LREC 2010), Malta, pp. 2868–2872 (2010)
5. Firat, O., Cho, K., Sankaran, B., Vural, F.T.Y., Bengio, Y.: Multi-way, multilingual neural machine translation. Comput. Speech Lang. **45**, 236–252 (2017)
6. Johnson, M., et al.: Google's multilingual neural machine translation system: enabling zero-shot translation. Trans. Assoc. Comput. Linguist. **5**, 339–351 (2017)
7. Junczys-Dowmunt, M., Dwojak, T., Hoang, H.: Is neural machine translation ready for deployment? A case study on 30 translation directions. In: Proceedings of the 9th International Workshop on Spoken Language Translation (IWSLT), Seattle, WA, pp. 1–8 (2016)
8. Koehn, P., Birch, A., Steinberger, R.: 462 machine translation systems for Europe. In: Proceedings of the Twelfth Machine Translation Summit, Denver, Colorado, USA, pp. 65–72 (2009)
9. Koehn, P., et al.: Moses: open source toolkit for statistical machine translation. In: Proceedings of the 45th Annual Meeting of the Association for Computational Linguistics, Prague, Czech Republic, pp. 177–180 (2007)
10. Lavie, A., Agarwal, A.: METEOR: an automatic metric for MT evaluation with high levels of correlation with human judgments. In: Proceedings of the Second Workshop on Statistical Machine Translation, StatMT 2007, Prague, Czech Republic, pp. 228–231 (2007)
11. Liu, S., Wang, L., Liu, C.H.: Chinese-Portuguese machine translation: a study on building parallel corpora from comparable texts. In: Proceedings of the Eleventh International Conference on Language Resources and Evaluation (LREC 2018), Miyazaki, Japan, pp. 1485–1494 (2018)
12. Miura, A., Neubig, G., Sudoh, K., Nakamura, S.: Tree as a pivot: syntactic matching methods in pivot translation. In: Proceedings of the Second Conference on Machine Translation, Volume 1: Research Paper, Copenhagen, Denmark, pp. 90–98 (2017)
13. Och, F.J.: Minimum error rate training in statistical machine translation. In: Proceedings of the 41st Annual Meeting on Association for Computational Linguistics, Sapporo, Japan, pp. 160–167 (2003)
14. Och, F.J., Ney, H.: A systematic comparison of various statistical alignment models. Comput. Linguist. **29**(1), 19–51 (2003)
15. Papineni, K., Roukos, S., Ward, T., Zhu, W.J.: BLEU: a method for automatic evaluation of machine translation. In: Proceedings of the 40th Annual Meeting on Association for Computational Linguistics, Philadelphia, PA, USA, pp. 311–318 (2002)

16. Sennrich, R., et al.: Nematus: a toolkit for neural machine translation. In: Proceedings of the Software Demonstrations of the 15th Conference of the European Chapter of the Association for Computational Linguistics, Valencia, Spain, pp. 65–68 (2017)
17. Sennrich, R., Haddow, B., Birch, A.: Neural machine translation of rare words with subword units. In: Proceedings of the 54th Annual Meeting of the Association for Computational Linguistics (Volume 1: Long Papers), ACL 2016, 7–12 August 2016, Berlin, Germany, pp. 1715–1725 (2016)
18. Snover, M., Dorr, B., Schwartz, R., Micciulla, L., Makhoul, J.: A study of translation edit rate with targeted human annotation. In: Proceedings of the 7th Biennial Conference of the Association for Machine Translation in the Americas (AMTA-2006), Cambridge, Massachusetts, USA, pp. 223–231 (2006)
19. Steinberger, R., et al.: The JRC-Acquis: a multilingual aligned parallel corpus with 20+ languages. In: Proceedings of the Fifth International Conference on Language Resources and Evaluation (LREC-2006), Genoa, Italy, pp. 2142–2147 (2006)
20. Stolcke, A.: SRILM - an extensible language modeling toolkit. In: Proceedings of the 7th International Conference on Spoken Language Processing, Colorado, USA, pp. 901–904 (2002)
21. Utiyama, M., Isahara, H.: A comparison of pivot methods for phrase-based statistical machine translation. In: Proceedings of Human Language Technologies, The Conference of the North American Chapter of the Association for Computational Linguistics (NAACL 2007), Rochester, USA, pp. 484–491 (2007)
22. Wang, M.H., Lei, C.L.: Boosting election prediction accuracy by crowd wisdom on social forums. In: 2016 13th IEEE Annual Consumer Communications & Networking Conference (CCNC), pp. 348–353. IEEE, Las Vegas (2016)
23. Wu, H., Wang, H.: Pivot language approach for phrase-based statistical machine translation. Mach. Transl. **21**(3), 165–181 (2007)
24. Zhang, J., et al.: THUMT: an open source toolkit for neural machine translation. arXiv preprint arXiv:1706.06415 (2017)
25. Zhu, X., He, Z., Wu, H., Wang, H., Zhu, C., Zhao, T.: Improving pivot-based statistical machine translation using random walk. In: Proceedings of the 2013 Conference on Empirical Methods in Natural Language Processing, Seattle, USA, pp. 524–534 (2013)
26. Ziemski, M., Junczys-Dowmunt, M., Pouliquen, B.: The united nations parallel corpus v1.0. In: Proceedings of The International Conference on Language Resources and Evaluation (LREC), Portorož, Slovenia, pp. 1–5 (2016)

Controlling the Transition of Hidden States for Neural Machine Translation

Zaixiang Zheng, Shujian Huang[✉], Xin-Yu Dai, and Jiajun Chen

Nanjing University, Nanjing 210023, People's Republic of China
{zhengzx,huangsj,daixy,chenjj}@nlp.nju.edu.cn

Abstract. Recurrent Neural Networks (RNN) based Neural Machine Translation (NMT) models under an encoder-decoder framework show significant improvements in translation quality recently. Given the encoded representations of source sentence, the NMT systems generate translated sentence word by word, dependent on the hidden states of the decoder. The hidden states of the decoder update at each decoding step, deciding the next translation to be generated. In this case, the transitions of the hidden states between successive steps contribute to the decisions of the next token of the translation, which draws less attention in previous work. In this work, we propose an explicit supervised objective on the transitions of the decoder hidden states, aiming to help our model to learn the transitional patterns better. We first attempt to model the increment of the transition by the proposed subtraction operation. Then, we require the increment to be predictive of the word to translate. The proposed approach strengthens the relationship between the transition of the decoder and the translation. Empirical evaluation shows considerable improvements on Chinese-English, German-English, and English-German translation tasks, demonstrating the effectiveness of our approach.

Keywords: Neural Machine Translation · Transition · Control

1 Introduction

Recently, neural network based methods show a promising trend in natural language processing, especially in the field of machine translation. Generally, a NMT adopts an *encoder-decoder* architecture with *attention mechanism* to model translating process [1,3,5,6,11,12]. Several approaches have been proposed to be the basic neural block of the encoder-decoder architecture, such as Recurrent Neural Networks (RNN) [1,11], Convolutional Neural Networks (CNN) [5] and self attention mechanism [12]. RNN-based models usually adopt a bi-directional RNNs as the encoder and a uni-directional RNNs as the decoder, both of which are bridged by the attention mechanism [1]. The encoder maps the source sentence into a set of continuous representations. Given the encoded source representations, the decoder generates the target sentence autoregressively.

© Springer Nature Singapore Pte Ltd. 2019
J. Chen and J. Zhang (Eds.): CWMT 2018, CCIS 954, pp. 86–92, 2019.
https://doi.org/10.1007/978-981-13-3083-4_8

The hidden states of the decoder RNNs maintain the translation semantics during the decoding process. Previous work shows that the contents of the hidden representations are predictive of several linguistic attributes [4]. The hidden states model the span-level information of the decoding process, which updates with regard to the translation to be generated in each time step. In each decoding step, the decoder hidden states are able to predict the rest untranslated word sets dynamically for each step [13]. Zheng et al. [14] assume that the information of the decoder hidden states may maintain both translated and untranslated contents, which are varied according to the translation process. This evidence implies the important role of the hidden state's transition to the translation decision, say, the increment of successive hidden states.

The original training objective, i.e. MLE (Maximum Likelihood Estimation), focuses on overall target conditional likelihood, not directly controlling the transition of the decoder hidden states. It probably makes NMT fail to learn a model with better transitional manner. Hence, an explicit guidance is supposed to help the NMT to strengthen the transition of the hidden states.

In this work, we propose an explicit supervision to control the transition of the decoder hidden state in the learning process. We first attempt to model the increment of the transition by proposed subtraction operation, then require the increment to be predictive of the word to translate. The proposed approach strengthens the relationship between the transition of the decoder and the translation.

Experiments show that our proposed model obtain considerable improvements in BLEU score over an attention-based NMT baseline on Chinese to English, German to English, and English to German translation tasks, demonstrating the importance of the transition of decoder hidden states in RNN-based NMT and the necessity in explicit control on the transition.

2   Neural Machine Translation

Given a source sentence as $\mathbf{x} = \{x_1, \ldots, x_I\}$, and a target sentence as $\mathbf{y} = \{y_1, \ldots, y_T\}$, the NMT models the translation probabilities from the source sentence to the target sentence:

$$P(\mathbf{y}|\mathbf{x}) = \prod_{t=1}^{T} P(y_t|y_{<t}, \mathbf{x}) \tag{1}$$

In the t-th decoding step, the word translation is generated according to the probability as follows:

$$P(y_t|y_{<t}, \mathbf{x}) = \mathrm{softmax}(g(y_{t-1}, \mathbf{s}_t, \mathbf{c}_t)) \tag{2}$$

where $g(\cdot)$ is a non-linear activation function; y_{t-1} is the output word from time step $t-1$; $\mathbf{s}_t$ is the current *decoding state*; the transition between decoding states is modeled as:

$$\mathbf{s}_t = f(y_{t-1}, \mathbf{s}_{t-1}, \mathbf{c}_t) \tag{3}$$

where $f(\cdot)$ is the RNN unit, $\mathbf{c}_t$ is the corresponding source context vector from the attention mechanism:

$$\mathbf{c}_t = \sum_{i=1}^{I} \alpha_{t,i} \cdot \mathbf{h}_i \tag{4}$$

$$\alpha_{t,i} = \mathrm{softmax}\big(a(\mathbf{s}_{t-1}, \mathbf{h}_i)\big) \tag{5}$$

where $a(\cdot)$ is the attention model for the relation between $\mathbf{s}_{t-1}$ and the encoder state $\mathbf{h}_i$.

3 Controlling the Transition of Decoder Hidden States

As typical RNN decoder generates target sentence word by word, the latent semantic representations maintained by the decoder hidden states gradually vary in the wake of the transition of the decoding state. For clarity, let us take $\{\mathbf{s}_{t-1}, \mathbf{s}_t\}$ and y_t for example. Since $\mathbf{s}_t$ is obtained from $\mathbf{s}_{t-1}$ by Eq. (3), we denote $\boldsymbol{\Delta}\mathbf{s}_t$ as the variation from $\mathbf{s}_{t-1}$ to $\mathbf{s}_t$. Intuitively, the transition of two successive decoder hidden states should be in accordance with what should be predicted in the current time-step, since the current state is updated by the current attentive context $\mathbf{c}_t$. Otherwise, it might be vague to tell what should this transition contribute to. Hence, the relation between the transition and the translation could be formulated as $\boldsymbol{\Delta}\mathbf{s}_t \approx y_t$ (Fig. 1).

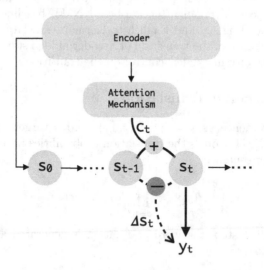

Fig. 1. Illustration of proposed approach. Dotted lines denote the proposed subtraction and predictive constraint.

Formally, we apply a predictive constraint to require the increment of the hidden states being predictive of the to-be-translated word. It is expected to explicitly enhance the consistency between $\boldsymbol{\Delta}\mathbf{s}_t$ and y_t:

$$q(y_t|\Delta s_t) = \text{softmax}\left(\mathbf{E}(y_t)^\top \mathbf{W}\Delta s_t\right) \tag{6}$$

where $\mathbf{W}$ is a learned matrix.

3.1 Modeling Transition

We propose two approaches to model the increment of the decoder state Δs_t.

- **Algebraic Subtraction:** It is a general assumption that the decoding states form a shared latent representation space. Hence we can directly by obtaining Δs_t an algebraic subtraction operation:

$$\Delta s_t = s_t - s_{t-1} \tag{7}$$

- **Parametric Subtraction:** We can alternately apply the subtraction in a parametric manner where the subtrahend and minuend are first mapped by separate linear transformations $\mathbf{U}_1$ and $\mathbf{U}_2$, respectively:

$$\Delta s_t = \mathbf{U}_1 s_t - \mathbf{U}_2 s_{t-1} \tag{8}$$

3.2 Training

We add the proposed predictive loss on transitions for one sentence:

$$q_\gamma(\mathbf{y}) = \sum_t^T q(y_t|\Delta s_t) \tag{9}$$

$q_\gamma(\mathbf{y})$ is the proposed predictive loss on sentence level. γ is the corresponding parameters to learn. We let $q_\gamma(\mathbf{y})$ be a additional regularized term to the training objective. Accordingly, given the training sentence pairs $\{[\mathbf{x}^{(m)}, \mathbf{y}^{(m)}]\}_{m=1}^M$, the new training objective is:

$$\mathcal{L}(\theta, \gamma) = \arg\max_{\theta, \gamma} \frac{1}{M} \sum_{m=1}^M \log P_\theta(\mathbf{y}^{(m)}|\mathbf{x}^{(m)})$$
$$+ \log q_\gamma(\mathbf{y}^{(m)}) \tag{10}$$

3.3 Rescoring in Testing

Since Δs_t is supposed to predict y_t, we can employ $P(y_t|y_{<t}) + q(y_t|\Delta s_t)$ instead of typical $P(y_t|y_{<t})$ as the search score in testing phase. This *rescoring* strategy ensure the consistence of the objectives between the training and testing. Empirical evaluation shows the effectiveness of the rescoring.

4   Experiment

We conduct experiments on both Chinese-English (Zh-En), German-English (De-En), and English-German (En-De) translation tasks. For Zh-En, our training dataset consists of 1.34 million sentence pairs extracted from LDC[1]. We choose NIST 2003 (MT03) dataset as our development set; NIST 2004 (MT04), 2005 (MT05) datasets as our test sets. Our models are trained on the sentences with a maximum length of 80 words. We limit the vocabulary size to 30K. For De-En and En-De, we conduct our experiments on the WMT17 [2] corpus. The dataset consists of 5.6M sentence pairs. We use newstest2016 as our development set, and newstest2017 as our testset. We follow [8] to segment both German and English words into subwords using byte-pair encoding [10, BPE]. Our models are trained on the sentences with a maximum length of 50 words. We use the total BPE vocabulary for each side. We measure the translation quality by BLEU scores [7].

We develop our method based on an attention-based NMT, which is an open source implementation of Nematus [9].

5   Results on Zh-En Task

We investigate the effects of different kinds of subtraction and reordering of our proposed approach. We list BLEU scores of our proposed models in Table 1. We compare the BLEU scores of our models with an attention-based NMT baseline (RNNSEARCH).

Table 1. Case-insensitive BLEU on Zh-En translation task. "rescoring" means using the same score function as training in testing phase (Sect. 3.3).

#	Model	MT03	MT04	MT05	Avg.	Δ
0	RNNSEARCH	37.95	40.80	36.06	38.27	–
1	*Algebraic subtraction*	38.66	40.93	37.00	38.86	+0.59
2	*Parametric subtraction*	39.07	41.23	37.35	39.22	+0.95
3	*Algebraic subtraction* + rescoring	39.53	41.88	37.40	39.60	+1.33
4	*Parametric subtraction* + rescoring	39.95	42.53	38.17	40.22	+1.95

5.1   Translation Quality

As shown in Table 1, the proposed models outperform RNNSEARCH baseline system in all datasets, which verifies that the explicit control on the transition of the decoder hidden state is effective.

---

[1] The corpora includes LDC2002E18, LDC2003E07, LDC2003E14, Hansards portion of LDC2004T07, LDC2004T08 and LDC2005T06.

Transition Modeling. Both kinds of subtraction for modeling transition improve the translation quality. Algebraic subtraction increases +0.59 BLEU score while 0.87 for parametric subtraction. The parametric subtraction is more generic and more expressive, giving the model more flexibility to the minus operation between two hidden states. Furthermore, note that in the testing phase, the computation of our models is exactly the same as the baseline model. These results indicate that the proposed transitional control bring benefits to the model learning, leading to better model parameters.

Effect of Rescoring. Using rescoring in testing phase could obtain higher 1.95 BLEU points, demonstrating the benefit of using the same score function in both training and testing time. It also indicates that the transition of the implies the information of next predicted word as our expectation.

5.2 Parameters and Speeds

The proposed subtractions mechanism require few increases of parameters. It somewhat slows the speed in training phase mainly because we employ extra softmax layer. Since the forward process of our models is the same as the baseline model, our models do not affect the speed in testing time. Using rescoring in testing obtains better translation quality but affects the efficiency of the decoding (Table 2).

Table 2. Statistics of parameters, training and testing speeds (sentences per second).

Model	#Parameter	Speed	
		Train	Test
RNNSEARCH	80M	42.59	2.05
Algebraic subtraction	80.5M	37.91	2.03
Parametric subtraction	82.5M	36.50	2.00
Parametric subtraction + reordering	82.5M	36.55	1.72

6 Results on De-En and En-De Tasks

As shown in Table 3, we find our proposed models also obtain considerable improvements on De-En and En-De translation tasks, respectively. This shows that our proposed method's effectiveness across different language pairs. Note that the En-De and De-En experiments are conducted on BPE units, where semantic granularity is different from typical word-based NMT systems, It indicates the compatibility of our method on control the transition of the hidden state in sub-word level.

Table 3. Case-sensitive BLEU on De-En and En-De Translation Tasks.

Model	De-En		En-De	
	Dev	Test	Dev	Test
RNNSEARCH	32.0	27.8	28.3	23.3
Parametric subtraction	32.2	28.7	29.6	23.6
Parametric subtraction + rescoring	32.9	29.1	30.6	24.1

7 Conclusion

In this paper, we propose to explicitly control the transition of the decoder hidden states. We introduce two kinds of semantic subtraction to obtain the increment of the decoder hidden states and require the increment being predictive of current translation as an explicit supervision. Experiments show the benefit by employing the additional supervisions on the transition of the decoder hidden state.

References

1. Bahdanau, D., Cho, K., Bengio, Y.: Neural machine translation by jointly learning to align and translate. In: ICLR 2015 (2015)
2. Bojar, O., et al. (eds.): Proceedings of the Second Conference on Machine Translation. Association for Computational Linguistics, Copenhagen, September 2017. http://www.aclweb.org/anthology/W17-47
3. Cho, K., et al.: Learning phrase representations using RNN encoder-decoder for statistical machine translation. In: EMNLP 2014 (2014)
4. Conneau, A., Kruszewski, G., Lample, G., Barrault, L., Baroni, M.: What you can cram into a single vector: probing sentence embeddings for linguistic properties (2018). http://arxiv.org/abs/1805.01070
5. Gehring, J., Auli, M., Grangier, D., Yarats, D., Dauphin, Y.: Convolutional sequence to sequence learning. In: ICML 2017 (2017)
6. Luong, T., Pham, H., Manning, D.C.: Effective approaches to attention-based neural machine translation. In: EMNLP 2015 (2015)
7. Papineni, K., Roukos, S., Ward, T., Zhu, W.J.: BLEU: a method for automatic evaluation of machine translation. In: ACL 2002 (2002)
8. Sennrich, R., et al.: The University of Edinburgh's neural MT systems for WMT17 (2017)
9. Sennrich, R., et al.: Nematus: A Toolkit for Neural Machine Translation (2016)
10. Sennrich, R., Haddow, B., Birch, A.: Neural machine translation of rare words with subword units. Comput. Sci. (2016)
11. Sutskever, I., Vinyals, O., Le, Q.V.: Sequence to sequence learning with neural networks. In: NIPS 2014 (2014)
12. Vaswani, A., et al.: Attention is all you need. In: NIPS 2017. Curran Associates, Inc. (2017)
13. Weng, R., Huang, S., Zheng, Z., Dai, X.Y., Chen, J.: Neural machine translation with word predictions. In: EMNLP 2017 (2017)
14. Zheng, Z., et al.: Modeling Past and Future for Neural Machine Translation. ArXiv e-prints, November 2017

Neural Name Translation Improves Neural Machine Translation

Xiaoqing Li[1,2], Jinghui Yan[4(✉)], Jiajun Zhang[1,2], and Chengqing Zong[1,2,3]

[1] National Laboratory of Pattern Recognition, Institute of Automation, CAS,
Beijing, China
{xqli,jjzhang,cqzong}@nlpr.ia.ac.cn
[2] University of Chinese Academy of Sciences, Beijing, China
[3] CAS Center for Excellence in Brain Science and Intelligence Technology,
Beijing, China
[4] Beijing Jiaotong University, Beijing, China
17112083@bjtu.edu.cn

Abstract. In order to control computational complexity, neural machine translation (NMT) systems convert all rare words outside the vocabulary into a single unk symbol. Previous solution (Luong et al. [1]) resorts to use multiple numbered unks to learn the correspondence between source and target rare words. However, testing words unseen in the training corpus cannot be handled by this method. And it also suffers from the noisy word alignment. In this paper, we focus on a major type of rare words – named entity (NE), and propose to translate them with character level sequence to sequence model. The NE translation model is further used to derive high quality NE alignment in the bilingual training corpus. With the integration of NE translation and alignment modules, our NMT system is able to surpass the baseline system by 2.9 BLEU points on the Chinese to English task.

Keywords: Rare words · Named entity · Neural machine translation

1 Introduction

Neural machine translation is a recently proposed approach to MT and has shown competing results to conventional translation methods (Kalchbrenner and Blunsom [2]; Cho et al. [3]; Sutskever et al. [4]). Despite several advantages over conventional methods, such as no domain knowledge requirement, better generalization to novel translations and less memory consumption, it has a significant weakness in handling rare words. In order to control computational complexity, NMT systems convert all rare words outside the vocabulary into a single unk symbol. Such conversion makes them unable to translate rare words. And those meaningless unks also increase the difficulty for the NMT model to learn the correspondence between source and target words.

To tackle this problem, Luong et al. [1] propose to augment the unk symbol with alignment information. Their method allow the NMT system to learn, for

© Springer Nature Singapore Pte Ltd. 2019
J. Chen and J. Zhang (Eds.): CWMT 2018, CCIS 954, pp. 93–100, 2019.
https://doi.org/10.1007/978-981-13-3083-4_9

each unk in the target sentence, the position of its corresponding word in the source sentence. A post-processing step is adopted to translate target unks with a dictionary.

This approach has been shown effective to handle rare words, but there are still some drawbacks. First, it cannot translate words outside the dictionary. Second, it relies on noisy word alignment. As known to all, automatic word alignment for rare words is far from perfect. Wrong alignment will reduce the quality of the bilingual corpus to train NMT model, and the dictionary extracted according to word alignment will also be noisy. Third, the content of rare words is totally ignored. Taking the following sentence as an example,

Judy chases the pat with unk.

The translation of this sentence into Chinese will be quite different depending on whether the last word is a person name or a modifier describing some feature of the pat.

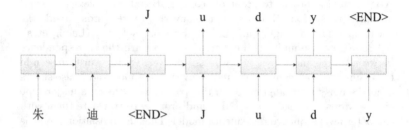

Fig. 1. Character level sequence to sequence model for NE translation.

To solve the above problems, we propose to translate rare words with character level sequence to sequence model, as shown in Fig. 1. Due to the limitation of existing resources, we limit our research in this paper to a major type of rare words – named entities. With an NE translator trained on external NE list, we can derive high quality NE alignment in the bilingual corpus, from which more NE pairs can be extract to further enhance the NE translator. Similar to Luong et al. [1], the aligned NE pairs are then replaced with their type symbols and an NMT model is trained on the new data. A post-processing step is employed to recover the translation of the replaced NEs.

Our experiments demonstrate the effectiveness of this approach. Evaluation on the Chinese to English translation task shows that our integrated system surpasses the baseline system by 2.9 BLEU points, and brings an improvement of 1.6 BLEU points over Luong's method.

2   Named Entity Translation and Alignment Model

Figure 2 gives an overview of the architecture of our system. In the training phase, we first train a neural NE translation system with a characterlevel

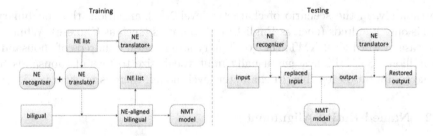

Fig. 2. System architecture to incorporate NE translation into neural MT.

sequence to sequence model. The initial training data consists of NE translation pairs, which can be obtained easily for many language pairs from the web. For example, we can extract linked Wikipedia titles and filter them according to category information. Then this NE translator together with a NE recognizer are used to find aligned NE pairs in the bilingual corpus. A list of NE pairs can be extracted from this corpus and it is combined with the original list to build a stronger NE translator. The aligned NE pairs in the bilingual corpus will be replaced with corresponding type symbols, resulting in sentence pairs like the following example,

ZH: LOC1 重新开放驻 LOC2 大使馆
EN: LOC1 reopens embassy in LOC2

Finally, this new data after replacement will be used to train an NMT model. In the testing phase, the NEs in the input sentence are first recognized and replaced with type symbols. After translated by the NMT model, the NE symbols in the output will be replaced with the translation of original NEs, which is generated by the NE translation module.

2.1 Named Entity Translator

The model we adopt to translate NE is a character level sequence to sequence model. It maps a source NE $s = (s_1, s_2, ..., s_m)$ into a target NE $t = (t_1, t_2, ..., t_n)$ with a single neural network as follows,

$$p(t|s) = \prod_{i-1}^{n} p(t_i|t_{<i}, s) \tag{1}$$

where the conditional probability is paramiterized with the encoder decoder framework. The encoder reads the source character sequence and encodes it into a sequence of hidden states. Then the decoder generates the target NE character by character based on the target hidden states. In this paper, we adopt the implementation of Bahdanau et al. [5] which introduces an attention mechanism while predicting each unit in target sequence. Please look into it for more detail. As pointed out by previous work, the total computational complexity will grow almost proportional to the target vocabulary in the sequence to sequence model.

Fortunately, in the scenario of character level NE translation, the vocabulary size is only hundreds (such as English) to thousands (such as Chinese). While in the case of word level NMT, the vocabulary size is often hundreds of thousands to millions. So NMT systems usually limit vocab size to tens of thousands to make computation feasible. In character level model, there is no such need.

2.2   Named Entity Alignment

Named entity alignment based on bilingual corpus alone is a hard task. Since a lot of NEs appear only a few times in the corpus, we cannot collect enough statistical evidence to infer reliable alignments with traditional word alignment model. Previous work (Huang et al. [6]; Feng et al. [7]) design multiple features, including translation score, transliteration score, distortion score etc., and use iterative training to discover aligned NEs in bilingual corpus.

However, if we have a high quality and high coverage NE list, together with a powerful NE translation model, things could be much easier. Inspired by Cambria et al. [21], which developed a Chinese common and common sense knowledge by using machine translation to translate some existing English common knowledge content into Chinese, we can learn a NE translator from the list, then use it to translate recognized NEs in one language and compare it with word sequence (up to trigram) in the other language. The longest common subsequence between NE translation candidate and target word sequence is adopted for similarity matching in this paper,

$$LCS(c, s) = \frac{1}{2}(|c| + |t| - ED(c, t)) \tag{2}$$

$$sim(c, t) = LCS(c, t)/|c| \tag{3}$$

where ED is the edit distance and $|x|$ is the length of x. For example, the longest common subsequence between 'bolin' and 'berlin' is 'blin'.

The final NE alignment result is the union of bi-directional matching, i.e. matching source NE with target word sequence and vice versa. We do not match bilingual NEs directly because the automatic NE recognition is not good enough and some NEs are not recognized in each language.

It has to mention that we don't have a list of numerical and temporal expressions to train a corresponding translation model before alignment. To calculate the similarity score, we carry the following conversion for both Chinese and English numerical expression,

- Convert Chinese and English numbers one to nine to abric numbers, discard all other characters. For example, '百分之四点二' (4.2%) will be converted into 42, and 4,200 will also be converted into 42.
- Add a few rules to handle exceptions such as month.

The above conversion is used for the sake of alignment. After NE pairs are extracted according to the alignment, they are used to train the NE translation model to handle NEs in testing data.

3   Experiments

We evaluate our method on the Chinese to English translation task. Translation quality is measured by the BLEU metric (Papineni et al., [8]).

3.1   Settings

The bilingual data to train the NMT model is selected from LDC, which contains about 0.6M sentence pairs. To avoid spending too much training time on long sentences, all sentence pairs longer than 50 words either on the source side or on the target side are discarded. The initial NE pairs are extracted from the Wikipedia, which consist about 350k entries. We use an in-house developed NE recognizer for Chinese and Stanford NER (Finkel et al. [9]) for English.

The NIST 03 dataset is chosen as the development set, which is used to monitoring the training process and decide the early stop condition. And the NIST 04 to 06 are used as our testing set.

3.2   Training Details

The hyperparameters used in our network are described as follows. We limit both the source and target vocabulary to 30k in our experiments. Names inside the vocabulary are not handled. The number of hidden units is 1,000 for both the encoder and decoder. And the embedding dimension is 500 for all source and target tokens. The network parameters are updated with the adadelta algorithm and the learning rate is set to 10^{-4}. The above setting is used both in the character level NE translation and word level sentence translation.

3.3   Name Translation and Alignment Performance

Because the recognition performance and crosslingual consistency are not good for organization names, we ignore this type and only handle numerical/temporal expressions, person names and location names in this paper. To evaluate the NE translation performance, we randomly extract 100 instances from the NIST testing data for each type, and manually find their translations in the reference. Whereas the NE alignment performance is evaluated on the same amount of samples extracted from the training data. The results are shown in Table 1.

Table 1. Translation and alignment performance with neural NE translation model

	N/T	PER	LOC
Translation	0.71	0.28	0.35
Trans. + lex. table	0.78	0.48	0.70
Alignment	0.97	0.93	0.96

It could be seen from the table that the translation accuracy is relatively low. Since accuracy is calculated in word level, the NE translation is regarded wrong even when there is only one letter different. In order to improve the NE translation accuracy in the post-processing step, we propose to use the lexical table extracted from the bilingual data if the NE could be found, otherwise the neural NE translation model will be used. On the other hand, the alignment accuracy is quite high. And most alignment errors relate to wrong word segmentation or NE recognition according to our investigation.

3.4   Sentence Translation Performance

We compare the translation performance of our method with that of Luong et al. [1]. The results are shown in Table 2. The baseline system we adopt is the attention-based model proposed in Bahdanau et al. [5]. It can be seen that only replacing rare NEs with our method results in a better performance than replacing all rare words with Luong's method. After combining the two methods, i.e., replacing NEs with our method and replacing other rare words with Luong's method, we could obtain an extra performance boost of 0.75 BLEU points, and the final performance surpass the baseline by 2.9 BLEU points on average. It has to be mentioned that Luong's method is not as effective on the Chinese-English language pair as reported on the French-English language pair. A possible reason is the automatic word alignment quality is worse on the former language pair. Moreover, we suspect that reordering could also be an influential factors of translation quality, due to the tags may damage the original sentence structures. We plan to incorporate a sentence type-based reordering model (Zhang et al. [19]) to handle the tags reording problem and find other influential factors in the future.

Table 2. Translation results for different systems

System	03 (dev)	04	05	06	Average
Baseline	25.65	28.94	25.13	27.86	26.90
Unk rep.	27.63	30.02	26.42	28.72	28.20
NE rep.	27.90	30.67	28.20	29.42	29.05
Unk+NE rep.	**29.01**	**31.33**	**28.80**	**30.08**	**29.80**

4   Related Work

Inability to handle rare words is a significant defect of NMT systems. And it has attracted much attention recently. Besides the work of Luong [1], Jean et al. [10] propose to directly use large vocabulary with a method based on importance sampling. As pointed out in their paper, their method is complementary and can be used together with replacement methods. Sennrich et al. [11] propose to represent rare words as sequences of subword units, and compares different techniques to segment words into subwords. Ling et al. [12] use a hierarchical structure for NMT, in which word representations are derived from character representations. Zhang et al. [20] feed the pseudo-parallel sentences synthesized by an additional bilingual dictionary into the training of NMT in order to translate low-frequency words or phrases.

The problem of NE translation has been studied for a long time. Knight and Graehl [13] study it with probabilistic finite-state transducers. Li et al. [14] present a joint source-channel model for direct orthographical mapping without intermediate phonemic representation. Freitag and Khadivi [15] propose a technique which combines conventional MT methods with a single layer perceptron. Deselaers et al. [16] use deep belief networks for machine transliteration. There are also some previous works trying to integrate NE translation into traditional MT systems. Hermjakob et al. [17] study the problem of "when to transliterate". Li et al. [18] propose to combine two copies of training data, the original one and the one with aligned NEs replaced.

5 Conclusion

In this paper, we enhance the ability of NMT system to handle rare words by incorporating NE translation and alignment modules. With the help of extra NE list and NE recognizer, our method is able to produce high quality NE alignments, and thus improves the data quality to train NE translation and sentence translation model. Experimental results show that our approach can significantly improve the translation performance.

Acknowledgement. The research work described in this paper has been supported by the National Key Research and Development Program of China under Grant No. 2016QY02D0303 and the Natural Science Foundation of China under Grant No. 61673380.

References

1. Luong, M.T., Sutskever, I., Le, Q.V., Vinyals, O., Zaremba, W.: Addressing the rare word problem in neural machine translation. arXiv preprint arXiv:1410.8206 (2014)
2. Kalchbrenner, N., Blunsom, P.: Recurrent continuous translation models. In: Proceedings of the 2013 Conference on Empirical Methods in Natural Language Processing, pp. 1700–1709 (2013)
3. Cho, K., et al.: Learning phrase representations using RNN encoder-decoder for statistical machine translation. arXiv preprint arXiv:1406.1078 (2014)
4. Sutskever, I., Vinyals, O., Le, Q.V.: Sequence to sequence learning with neural networks. In: Advances in Neural Information Processing Systems, pp. 3104–3112 (2014)

5. Bahdanau, D., Cho, K., Bengio, Y.: Neural machine translation by jointly learning to align and translate. arXiv preprint arXiv:1409.0473 (2014)
6. Huang, F., Vogel, S., Waibel, A.: Automatic extraction of named entity translingual equivalence based on multi-feature cost minimization. In: Proceedings of the ACL 2003 Workshop on Multilingual and Mixed-language Named Entity Recognition, pp. 9-16 (2003)
7. Feng, D., Lv, Y., Zhou, M.: A new approach for English-Chinese named entity alignment. In: Proceedings of the 2004 Conference on Empirical Methods in Natural Language Processing, pp. 372–379 (2004)
8. Papineni, K., Roukos, S., Ward, T., Zhu, W.J.: BLEU: a method for automatic evaluation of machine translation. In: Proceedings of the 40th Annual Meeting on Association for Computational Linguistics, pp. 311-318. Association for Computational Linguistics (2002)
9. Finkel, J.R., Grenager, T., Manning, C.: Incorporating non-local information into information extraction systems by Gibbs sampling. In: Proceedings of the 43rd Annual Meeting on Association for Computational Linguistics, pp. 363-370. Association for Computational Linguistics (2005)
10. Jean, S., Cho, K., Memisevic, R., Bengio, Y.: On using very large target vocabulary for neural machine translation. arXiv preprint arXiv:1412.2007 (2014)
11. Sennrich, R., Haddow, B., Birch, A.: Neural machine translation of rare words with subword units. arXiv preprint arXiv:1508.07909 (2015)
12. Ling, W., Trancoso, I., Dyer, C., Black, A.W.: Character-based neural machine translation. arXiv preprint arXiv:1511.04586 (2015)
13. Knight, K., Graehl, J.: Machine transliteration. Comput. Linguist. **24**(4), 599–612 (1998)
14. Li, H., Zhang, M., Su, J.: A joint source-channel model for machine transliteration. In: Proceedings of the 42nd Annual Meeting on Association for Computational Linguistics, pp. 159-166 (2004)
15. Freitag, D., Khadivi, S.: A sequence alignment model based on the averaged perceptron. In: Proceedings of the 2007 Joint Conference on Empirical Methods in Natural Language Processing and Computational Natural Language Learning, pp. 238-247 (2007)
16. Deselaers, T., Hasan, S., Bender, O., Ney, H.: A deep learning approach to machine transliteration. In: Proceedings of the Fourth Workshop on Statistical Machine Translation, Association for Computational Linguistics, pp. 233-241 (2009)
17. Hermjakob, U., Knight, K., Daumé III, H.: Name translation in statistical machine translation-learning when to transliterate. In: Proceedings of ACL 2008: HLT, pp. 389–397 (2008)
18. Li, H., Zheng, J., Ji, H., Li, Q., Wang, W.: Name-aware machine translation. In: Proceedings of the 51st Annual Meeting of the Association for Computational Linguistics, pp. 604–614 (2013)
19. Zhang, J., Zong, C., Li, S.: Sentence type based reordering model for statistical machine translation. In: Proceedings of the 22nd International Conference on Computational Linguistics, Vol. 1, pp. 1089-1096. Association for Computational Linguistics (2008)
20. Zhang J, Zong C.: Bridging neural machine translation and bilingual dictionaries. arXiv preprint arXiv:1610.07272 (2016)
21. Cambria, E., Hussain, A., Durrani, T., Zhang, J.: Towards a Chinese common and common sense knowledge base for sentiment analysis. In: Jiang, H., Ding, W., Ali, M., Wu, X. (eds.) IEA/AIE 2012. LNCS (LNAI), vol. 7345, pp. 437–446. Springer, Heidelberg (2012). https://doi.org/10.1007/978-3-642-31087-4_46

Towards Building a Strong Transformer Neural Machine Translation System

Qiang Wang[1,2], Bei Li[1], Jiqiang Liu[1], Bojian Jiang[1], Zheyang Zhang[1],
Yinqiao Li[1,2], Ye Lin[1], Tong Xiao[1,2(✉)], and Jingbo Zhu[1,2]

[1] Natrual Language Processing Lab, Northeastern University, Shenyang, China
{libeinlp,liujiqiang,jiangbojian,zhangzheyang,liyinqiao,
linyeneu}@stumail.neu.edu.cn, {xiaotong,zhujingbo}@mail.neu.edu.cn
[2] NiuTrans Inc., Shenyang, China
wangqiangneu@gmail.com

Abstract. Transformer model based on self-attention mechanism [17] has achieved state-of-the-art in recent evaluations. However, it is still unclear how much room there is for improvement of the translation system based on this model. In this paper we further explore how to build a stronger neural machine system from four aspects, including architectural improvements, diverse ensemble decoding, reranking, and postprocessing. Experimental results on CWMT-18 Chinese ↔ English tasks show that our approach can consistently improve the translation performance of 2.3–3.8 BLEU points than the strong baseline. Particularly, we find that ensemble decoding with a large number of diverse models is crucial for significant improvement.

1 Introduction

Neural machine translation (NMT) exploits an encoder-decoder framework to model the whole translation process in an end-to-end fashion, and has achieved state-of-the-art performance in many language pairs [14,19]. Among various translation models, the Transformer model [17] based on self-attention mechanism has shown promising results in terms of both translation performance and training speed, compared with previous counterparts, such as GNMT [19] or ConvS2S [3].

Although Transformer has achieved great success, it is still unclear that how much room there is for further improvement of the translation system based on it. To answer this issue, we firstly build a strong single Transformer model equipping with some of the existing technologies as baseline. Concretely, we enhance the baseline with checkpoint ensemble [14] that averages the last N checkpoints of a single training run. To enable open-vocabulary translation, all the words are segmented via byte pair encoding (BPE) [13] for both Chinese and English. Also, we use back-translation technique [12] to leverage the rich monolingual resource. As a result, our baseline can achieve comparable performance with the best reported results in CWMT-17.

© Springer Nature Singapore Pte Ltd. 2019
J. Chen and J. Zhang (Eds.): CWMT 2018, CCIS 954, pp. 101–110, 2019.
https://doi.org/10.1007/978-981-13-3083-4_10

To exceed the strong baseline, we further explore to improve the system from four aspects, including architectural improvements, diverse ensemble decoding, reranking and post-processing. For architectural improvements, we add relu dropout and attention dropout to improve the generalization ability and increase the inner dimension of feed-forward neural network to enlarge the model capacity [4]. We also use the novel Swish activation function [8] and self-attention with relative positional representations [15]. Next, we explore more diverse ensemble decoding via increasing the number of models and using the models generated by different ways. Furthermore, at most 17 features tuned by MIRA [2] are used to rerank the N-best hypotheses. At last, a post-processing algorithmic is proposed to correct the inconsistent English literals between the source and target sentence. Through these techniques, we can achieve consistent improvement of 2.3–3.8 BLEU points over the baselines. Particularly, we find that ensemble decoding with a large number of diverse models is crucial for significant improvement.

2   The Transformer System

Unlike usual NMT models, Transformer does not require any recurrent units for modeling word sequences of arbitrary length. Instead, it resorts to self-attention and standard feed-forward networks for both encoder and decoder.

On the encoder side, there are L identical stacked layers. Each of them is composed of a self-attention sub-layer and a feed-forward sub-layer. The attention model used in Transformer is scaled dot-product attention[1]. Its output is fed into a position-wise feed-forward network. To ease training, layer normalization [1] and residual connection [5] are used for the output of each sub-layer: LayerNorm(x + sublayer(x)). Likewise, the decoder has another stack of L identical layers. It has an encoder-decoder attention sub-layer in addition to the two sub-layers used in each encoder layer.

Given this model, we can use the cross entropy loss as the training objective, and make the network learn to update parameters by stochastic gradient descend (SGD).

3   Improvements

We improve the baseline system from four aspects, including architectural improvements, ensemble decoding, reranking and post-processing.

---

[1] Given a sequence of vectors and a position i, the self-attention model computes the dot-product of the input vectors for each pair of positions (i, j), followed by a rescaling operation and Softmax. In this way, we have an attention score (or weight) for each (i, j). It is then used to generate the output by a weighted sum over all input vectors.

3.1   Architectural Improvements

Dropout. The original Transformer only uses residual dropout when the information flow is added between two adjacent layers/sublayers, while the dropouts in feed-forward neural network (e.g. relu dropout) and self attention weights (e.g. attention dropout) are not in use. In practice, we observed the consistent improvements than baseline when we set relu dropout to 0.1 and attention dropout to 0.1, thanks to the regularization effect to overcome the overfitting.

Table 1. Samples of the inconsistent translation of the constant literal between source and target sentence. The subword is split by "@@". The two samples are picked up from CWMT-18 test set.

Source:	19P@@ ass@@ p@@ ort
Translation:	so there is the Pas@@ port , which was released last September .
Post-Processing:	so there is the Passport , which was released last September .
Source:	Furious residents have savaged Sol@@ i@@ hull Council saying it was " useless at dealing with the problem ".
Translation:	Ł S@@ ol@@ i@@ h@@ ou@@ s@@ , " Ɨ Ł "
Post-Processing:	Ł Solihull , " Ɨ Ł "

Larger Feed-Forward Network. Limited by the size of GPU memory, we can not directly train a big Transformer model with the batch size as large as the base model. To solve this, we resort to increase the inner dimension (refer to d_{ff}) of feed-forward network while other settings stay the same. It is consistent with the finding of [4] that the transformer model can benefit from larger d_{ff}.

Swish Activation Function. The standard Transformer model has a nonlinear expression capability due to the use of Rectified Linear Unit (ReLU) activation function. Recently, [8] propose a new activation function called Swish by the network automatic search technique based on reinforcement-learning. They claim that Swish tends to work better than ReLU on deeper models and can transfer well to a number of challenging tasks. Formally, Swish is computed as:

$$Swish(x) = x \cdot sigmoid(\beta x),$$

where β is either a constant or a learnable parameter. In practice, we replace ReLU with Swish ($\beta = 1$) and do not change any other settings.

Relative Positional Representation. Transformer uses the absolute position encodings based on sinusoids of varying frequency, while [15] point out that the representations of relative position can yield consistent improvement over the absolute counterpart. They equip the representations of both key and value with some trainable parameters (e.g. a_{ij}^K, a_{ij}^V in [15]) when calculating the self attention. We re-implement this model, and use clipping distance $k = 16$ with the unique edge representations per layer and head. We use both the absolute and relative positional representations simultaneously.

3.2 Diverse Ensemble Decoding

Ensemble decoding is a widely used technique to boost the performance by integrating the predictions of several models, and has been proved effective in the WMT competitions [10,11,18]. Existing experimental results about ensemble decoding mainly concentrate upon a small number of models (e.g. 4 models [10,14,18]). Besides, the ensembled models generally lack of sufficient diversity, for example, [14] use the last N checkpoints of a single training run, while [18] use the same network architecture with different random initializations.

In this paper, we study the effects of more diverse ensemble decoding from two perspectives: the number of models and the diversity of integrated models. We explore at most 16 models for jointly decoding by allocating two models per GPU device in our C++ decoder. In addition to using different random seeds, the ensembled models are generated from more diverse ways, such as different training steps, model sizes and network architectures (see Sect. 3.1).

Every ensembled model is also assigned a weight to indicate the confidence of prediction. In practice, we simply assign the same weight 1.0 for each model. We also study the greedy tuning strategy (randomly initialize all weights firstly, then fix other weights and only tune one weight each time), while there is no significant improvement observed.[2]

3.3 Reranking

We apply the reranking module to pick up a potentially better hypothesis from the n-best generated by ensemble decoding. The used features for reranking include:

- TFs: Translation features. We totally use eight types of translation features, and each type can be represented as a tuple with four elements: (L_s, D_s, L_t, D_t), where $L_s, L_t \in \{ZH, EN\}$ denotes the language of source and target respectively, and $D_s, D_t \in \{L2R, R2L\}$ denotes the direction of source and target sequence respectively. For example, (ZH, L2R, EN, R2L) denotes a system trained on ordinal Chinese $\rightarrow$ reversed English.
- LM: 5-gram language model of target side[3].
- SM: Sentence similarity. The best hypothesis from the target R2L system is compared to each n-best hypothesis and used to generate a sentence similarity score based on the cosine of the two sentence vectors. The sentence vector is represented by the mean of all word embeddings.

---

[2] We do not use some more sophisticated tuning methods, such as MERT, MIRA, due to the expensive cost for ensemble decoding, especially with a large beam size.

[3] All language models are trained by KenLM [6].

Given the above features, we calculate the ranking score by a simple linear model. All weights are tuned on the development set via MIRA. The hypothesis with the highest ranking score is chosen as the refined translation.

3.4 Post-processing

Current NMT system generates the translation word by word[4], which is difficult to guarantee the consistency of some constant literals between source sentence and its translation.

In this section, we focus on the English literals in a Chinese sentence. For example, as shown in Table 1, the literal "Passport" in Chinese sentence is translated into "Pasport" wrongly, and a similar error happens between "Solihull" and its translation "Solihous".

Algorithm 1. Post-processing algorithmic for inconsistent English literals translation.

Input: S: source sentence; T: NMT translation;
Output: T': translation after post-processing
1: Initialize: $T' = T$, create $\mathbb{S}(x, y)$ saves the similarity between x and y
2: Get the set of English literals $\mathbb{EL}$ from Chinese sentence (either S or T)
3: **for** each English literal el in $\mathbb{EL}$ **do**
4:     **if** el not in T **then**
5:         **for** each y in the set of n-gram of T $(1 \leq n \leq 3)$ **do**
6:             $\mathbb{S}(el, y) = sim(el, y)$
7:         **end for**
8:     **end if**
9:     $y^* = argmax_y \mathbb{S}(el, y)$
10:     replace el with y^* in T'
11: **end for**

To solve this issue, we propose a post-processing method to correct the unmatched translations for the constant literals, as shown in Algorithm 1. The basic idea is that the English literals appearing in Chinese sentence must be contained in English sentence. The challenge is that how to align the correct literal with its wrong one. In practice, we compute the normalized edit distance as the similarity:

$$sim(x, y) = \frac{D(x, y)}{L_x}, \tag{1}$$

where $D(x, y)$ denotes the edit-distance between x and y, L_x is the length of x. Then, the most similar translated literal is recovered by the original one.

Since the number of Chinese sentences containing the English literals is relatively small, our approach can not significantly improve the BLEU, but we find that it is very effective for human evaluation.

---

[4] Actually it is subword by subword in this paper.

4 Experiments and Results

4.1 Implement Details

Our systems are based on Transformer [17] implemented on the Tensor2Tensor[5]. We use base Transformer model as described in [17]: 6 blocks in the encoder and decoder networks respectively (word representations of size 512, feed-forward layers with inner dimension 2048, 8 attention heads, residual dropout is set to 0.1). We use negative Maximum Likelihood Estimation (MLE) as loss function, and train all the models using Adam [7] with $\beta_1 = 0.9$, $\beta_2 = 0.98$, and $\epsilon = 10^{-9}$. The learning rate is scheduled as described in [17]: $lr = d^{-0.5} \cdot min(t^{-0.5}, t \cdot 4000^{-1.5})$, where d is the dimension of word embedding, t is the training step number. To enable the open-vocabulary translation, we use byte pair encoding (BPE) [13] for both Chinese and English. All the models are trained for 15 epochs on one machine with 8 NVIDIA 1080 Ti GPUs. We limit source and target tokens per batch to 4096 per GPU, resulting in approximate 25,000 source and 25,000 target tokens in one training batch. We also use checkpoint ensemble by averaging the last 15 checkpoints, which are saved at 10-minute intervals.

For evaluation, we use beam search with length normalization [19]. By default, we use beam size of 12, while the coefficient of length normalization is tuned on development set. We use the home-made C++ decoder as a more efficient alternative to the tensorflow implementation, which is also necessary for our diverse ensemble decoding (Sect. 3.2). The hypotheses with too many consecutive repeated tokens (e.g. beyond the count of the most frequent token in the source sentence) are removed. We report all experimental results on CWMT-18 development set by tokenized case-sensitive BLEU-4 metric[6].

Table 2. Statistics of the training data

Direction	Lang.	Sentences	Tokens	Ave. sentence length
ZH → EN	ZH	7.2M	130M	17.6
	EN	7.2M	134M	18.6
EN → ZH	EN	16.9M	505M	29.9
	ZH	16.9M	465M	27.5

---

[5] https://github.com/tensorflow/tensor2tensor/tree/v1.0.14. We choose this version because we found that this implementation is more similar to the original model described in [17] than newer versions.

[6] https://github.com/moses-smt/mosesdecoder/blob/master/scripts/generic/multi-bleu.perl.

4.2 Chinese → English Results

For Chinese → English task, we only use the CWMT corpus as training data. All texts are segmented by home-made word segmentation toolkit[7]. We remove the parallel sentence pairs which is duplicated, exceptional length ratio, or bad alignment score obtained by fast-align[8]. Detailed statistical information of training data is shown in Table 2. Then we learn BPE codes with 32k merge operations from independent Chinese and English text, resulting in the size of source and target vocabulary is 47K and 33K respectively. We also study the effect of merge operations, however no significant gain is found when we shrink or expand the number of merge operations.

Table 3. BLEU scores [%] on CWMT-18 development set for Chinese-English translation.

	System	beam size	Valid.
Baselines	Transformer-Base	12	24.40
	+checkpoint ensemble	12	24.93
Architecture	+d_{ff} =4096	12	25.31
	+dropout	12	25.75
	baseline+big	12	24.81
	baseline+swish	12	24.98
	baseline+rpr	12	25.21
	baseline+dropout	12	25.63
	baseline+swish+dropout	12	25.52
	baseline+rpr+dropout	12	25.60
Diverse Decoding	4 same models with different random seeds	12	27.40
	4 diverse models	12	27.51
	4 diverse models with large beam	100	27.64
	8 diverse models	100	27.91
	16 diverse models	80	28.12
Re-ranking	17 features	-	28.75
Post-processing	English literal revised	-	**28.76**

Table 3 presents the BLEU scores on CWMT-18 development set of Chinese → English task. First of all, we can see that using checkpoint ensemble brings +0.53 BLEU than the baseline of single model. When we equip the Transformer base model with larger d_{ff} and relu & attention dropout, +0.82 BLEU are improved further. However, to our disappointment, we do not observe consistent improvement via Swish or relative positional representations. Note that the big Transformer model with small batch size (e.g. 2048) even underperforms our baseline, which indicates that the batch size is an essential factor to train a good Transformer model. It is important to notice that although not all model

---

[7] For Chinese, the word segmentation is done based on unigram language model with Viterbi algorithm.

[8] https://github.com/clab/fast_align.

variants can improve the performance orthogonally, we can apply the diversity between these variants to improve other aspects (e.g. ensemble decoding).

Based on the strong single model baseline, we firstly study the conventional ensemble decoding: 4 models with different random seeds, resulting in a significant gain of 1.65 BLEU point. Then we use 4 models with different architectures: *baseline*, $d_{ff} = 4096$, *dropout* and $d_{ff} = 4096 +$ dropout, then an interesting result is that the diverse ensemble decoding is superior than the ensemble of $d_{ff} = 4096 + dropout$, which provides an evidence that diverse models may be more important than homogeneous strong models. The beam size of 100 is a bit better than 12. This result is inconsistent with previous work claiming that larger beam size can badly drop down the performance [16], which needs to be invested further. Additionally, we expand the number of models from 4 to 8 and 16^9, the overall performances are further improved +0.27 and +0.52 respectively. For 16 models ensemble decoding, we arrange every two models on one GPU via our C++ decoder.

Then we rerank the n-best from diverse ensemble decoding (at most 80 candidates) with 17 features[10], we achieve +0.57 BLEU improvement thanks to the complementary information brought by the features. At last, we do post-processing for the reranking output, but almost no effect on BLEU due to limited English literals are found in Chinese sentences (Table 4).

Table 4. BLEU scores [%] on CWMT-18 development set for English → Chinese translation.

	System	beam size	Valid.
Baselines	Transformer-Base	12	24.83
	+checkpoint ensemble	12	25.33
Architecture	+d_{ff}=4096	12	25.77
	+dropout	12	25.85
Diverse Decoding	4 same models with different random seeds	12	26.48
	4 diverse models	12	26.74
	4 diverse models + big beam	100	26.68
	10 diverse models	80	27.18
Re-ranking	4 features	-	27.51
Post-processing	English literal revised	-	**27.61**

4.3   English → Chinese Results

For English → Chinese translation, in addition to the CWMT corpus, we additionally uses part of UN and News-Commentary combined data and pseudo

---

[9] The types of used models include *baseline*, d_{ff}, *dropout*, $d_{ff} + dropout$, *Swish*, *RPR* (relative position representation), *big* (Transformer big model with small batch size) and baseline-epoch20 (training 20 epochs rather than 15).

[10] Seven (ZH, EN, L2R, L2R) models, four (ZH, EN, L2R, R2L) models, one (ZH, EN, R2L, L2R) feature, one (ZH, EN, R2L, R2L) feature, one (EN, ZH, R2L, L2R) feature, one (EN, ZH, R2L, R2L) feature, one LM feature, one SM feature.

parallel data from back-translation. The UN and News-Commentary combined data is selected by XenC [9][11] according to the *xmu* Chinese monolingual corpus from CWMT, and *xin_cmn* monolingual corpus is used for back-translation. Data preprocessing is same as Sect. 4.2, resulting in 7.2M CWMT corpus, 3.5M UN and News-Commentary combined corpus, and 6.2M pseudo parallel data. Then 32k merge operations are used for BPE.

Like Chinese $\rightarrow$ English, using checkpoint ensemble can bring a gain of +0.5 BLEU solidly. At the same time, increasing the dimension of d_{ff} and activate more dropout are proved effective again. The biggest difference from Chinese $\rightarrow$ English is that diverse ensemble decoding improves the performance at most +1.33 BLEU when we integrate 10 models. However, increasing either the number of models or the diversity is helpful for ensemble decoding. As for reranking, although we only use four (EN, ZH, L2R, R2L) models as features due to time constraint. there is still +0.33 BLEU improvement obtained. At last, post-processing makes an more obvious effect for English $\rightarrow$ Chinese translation than Chinese $\rightarrow$ English.

5   Conclusion

We build a strong Transformer neural machine translation system as baseline, and have achieved comparable performance than the CWMT-17 best ensembled results. Beyond the baseline, we further improve the performance from four aspects, including architectural improvements, diverse ensemble decoding, reranking and post-processing. Experimental results show that our approach can improve 2.3–3.8 BLEU points consistently. Particularly, we find that increasing the number of models and the diversity of models is crucial for ensemble decoding.

Acknowledgments. This work was supported in part by the National Science Foundation of China (No. 61672138 and 61432013), the Fundamental Research Funds for the Central Universities.

References

1. Ba, J.L., Kiros, R., Hinton, G.E.: Layer normalization. CoRR abs/1607.06450 (2016). http://arxiv.org/abs/1607.06450
2. Chiang, D., Marton, Y., Resnik, P.: Online large-margin training of syntactic and structural translation features, pp. 224–233. Association for Computational Linguistics (2008)
3. Gehring, J., Auli, M., Grangier, D., Yarats, D., Dauphin, Y.N.: Convolutional sequence to sequence learning. ArXiv e-prints, May 2017
4. Hassan, H., et al.: Achieving human parity on automatic Chinese to English news translation. arXiv preprint arXiv:1803.05567 (2018)

---

[11] https://github.com/antho-rousseau/XenC.

5. He, K., Zhang, X., Ren, S., Sun, J.: Identity mappings in deep residual networks. In: Leibe, B., Matas, J., Sebe, N., Welling, M. (eds.) ECCV 2016. LNCS, vol. 9908, pp. 630–645. Springer, Cham (2016). https://doi.org/10.1007/978-3-319-46493-0_38

6. Heafield, K.: KenLM: faster and smaller language model queries. In: Proceedings of the EMNLP 2011 Sixth Workshop on Statistical Machine Translation, Edinburgh, Scotland, United Kingdom, pp. 187–197, July 2011. https://kheafield.com/papers/avenue/kenlm.pdf

7. Kingma, D.P., Ba, J.: Adam: a method for stochastic optimization. arXiv preprint arXiv:1412.6980 (2014)

8. Ramachandran, P., Zoph, B., Le, Q.V.: Searching for activation functions (2018)

9. Rousseau, A.: Xenc: an open-source tool for data selection in natural language processing. Prague Bull. Math. Linguist. **100**, 73–82 (2013)

10. Sennrich, R., et al.: The University of Edinburgh's neural MT systems for WMT17. In: WMT 2017, pp. 389 (2017)

11. Sennrich, R., Haddow, B.: Linguistic input features improve neural machine translation. In: Proceedings of the First Conference on Machine Translation: Volume 1, Research Papers, pp. 83–91. Association for Computational Linguistics (2016)

12. Sennrich, R., Haddow, B., Birch, A.: Improving neural machine translation models with monolingual data. In: Proceedings of the 54th Annual Meeting of the Association for Computational Linguistics (Volume 1: Long Papers), vol. 1, pp. 86–96 (2016)

13. Sennrich, R., Haddow, B., Birch, A.: Neural machine translation of rare words with subword units. In: Proceedings of the 54th Annual Meeting of the Association for Computational Linguistics, ACL 2016, Volume 1: Long Papers, 7–12 August 2016, Berlin, Germany (2016). http://aclweb.org/anthology/P/P16/P16-1162.pdf

14. Sennrich, R., Haddow, B., Birch, A.: Edinburgh neural machine translation systems for WMT 16. In: Proceedings of the First Conference on Machine Translation: Volume 2, Shared Task Papers, pp. 371–376. Association for Computational Linguistics (2016)

15. Shaw, P., Uszkoreit, J., Vaswani, A.: Self-attention with relative position representations. In: Proceedings of the 2018 Conference of the North American Chapter of the Association for Computational Linguistics: Human Language Technologies, Volume 2 (Short Papers), vol. 2, pp. 464–468 (2018)

16. Tu, Z., Liu, Y., Shang, L., Liu, X., Li, H.: Neural machine translation with reconstruction. In: AAAI, pp. 3097–3103 (2017)

17. Vaswani, A., et al.: Attention is all you need. In: Advances in Neural Information Processing Systems, pp. 6000–6010 (2017)

18. Wang, Y., et al.: Sogou neural machine translation systems for WMT17. In: Proceedings of the Second Conference on Machine Translation, pp. 410–415 (2017)

19. Wu, Y., et al.: Google's neural machine translation system: bridging the gap between human and machine translation. arXiv preprint arXiv:1609.08144 (2016)

TencentFmRD Neural Machine Translation System

Bojie Hu[1(✉)], Ambyer Han[2], and Shen Huang[1]

[1] Tencent Research, Beijing, China
{bojiehu,springhuang}@tencent.com
[2] Natural Language Processing Lab, Northeastern University, Boston, USA
ambyerhan0301@outlook.com

Abstract. This paper describes the Neural Machine Translation (NMT) system of TencentFmRD. Our systems are neural machine translation systems trained with our original system TenTrans. TenTrans is an improved NMT system based on Transformer self-attention mechanism. In addition to the basic settings of Transformer training, TenTrans uses multi-model fusion techniques, multiple features reranking, different segmentation models and joint learning. Finally, we adopt some data selection strategies to fine-tune the trained system. Our English↔ Chinese and Mongolian→Chinese systems achieve a stable performance improvement.

Keywords: NMT · TenTrans · Self-attention
Multiple features reranking · Joint learning · Fine-tune

1 Introduction

End-to-end neural machine translation [1–5] based on self-attention mechanism [6], the Transformer, has become promising paradigm in field of machine translation academia and industry. Experiments show Transformer, which does not rely on any convolutional and recurrent networks, to be superior in translation performance while being more parallelizable and requiring significantly less time to train. The training part of this paper is an improvement on the tensor2tensor[1] open source project based on the Transformer architecture, and the inference part is completely original, and we called this system TenTrans.

This paper introduces our English↔Chinese and Mongolian→Chinese system in detail. We divide TenTrans system into three parts to introduce in this paper. First, we introduce how to train better translation model, that is, the training phase. Second, we describe how good models can generate better translation candidates, that is, the inference phase. Finally, we describe N-best rescoring phase, which ensures that translation results which are closer to the expression typically produced by users are chosen. Our experimental setup is based on recent

---

[1] https://github.com/tensorflow/tensor2tensor.

© Springer Nature Singapore Pte Ltd. 2019
J. Chen and J. Zhang (Eds.): CWMT 2018, CCIS 954, pp. 111–123, 2019.
https://doi.org/10.1007/978-981-13-3083-4_11

promising techniques in NMT, including using Byte Pair Encoding (BPE) [7] and mixed word/character segmentation rather than words as modeling units to achieve open-vocabulary translation [8], using back-translation [9] method and joint training [10] applied to make use of monolingual data to enhance training data. And we also improve the performance using an ensemble based on six variants of the same network, which are trained with different parameter settings.

In addition, we design a multi-dimensional features for strategic integration to select the best candidate from n-best translation lists. Then we perform minimum error rate training (MERT) [11] on validation set to give different features corresponding reasonable weights. And we process named entities, such as person name, location name and organization name into generalization types in order to improve the performance of unknown named entity translation [12]. Finally, we adopt some data selection strategies [13] to fine-tune the trained system and achieve a stable performance improvement.

Our English↔ Chinese and Mongolian→Chinese systems achieve a stable performance improvement. The remainder of this paper is organized as follows: Sect. 2 describes the system architecture of TenTrans. Section 3 states all experimental techniques in these systems. Section 4 shows designed features for reranking n-best lists. Section 5 shows experimental settings and results. Finally, we conclude in Sect. 6.

2   System Architecture of TenTrans

In this work, TenTrans has the same overall architecture as the Transformer: that is, it uses stacked self-attention and point-wise, fully connected layers for both the encoder and decoder. The encoder and decoder both are composed of a stack of $N = 6$ identical layers. Each layer has two sub-layers, multi-head self-attention mechanism and position-wise connected feed-forward network. We add a residual connection [15] around each of the two sub-layers, followed by layer normalization [16]. The left part of the first phase in Fig. 1 describes the structure of the basic sub-layer in the encoder and decoder. In addition to the two sub-layers in each encoder layer, the decoder inserts a third sub-layer, which performs multi-head attention over the output of the encoder stack. In this work we employ *mulithead* = 16 heads, that is, parallel attention layers. We use minimum likelihood estimation (MLE) to train TenTrans models.

For all our models, we adopt Adam [17] ($\beta_1 = 0.9$, $\beta_2 = 0.98$, $\epsilon = 10^{-9}$) as optimizer. Our learning rate changes dramatically with training process according to the formula:

$$lr = d_{model}^{-0.5} \cdot \min\left(update\_num^{-0.5}, update\_num \cdot warmup^{-1.5}\right) \quad (1)$$

where $d_{model} = 1024$ indicates model hidden state dimension, the same as input embedding dimension and output embedding dimension. We linearly increase the learning rate whose initial value is 0.1 in the first $warmup = 6000$ training steps, and then anneal according to Equation 1. We use synchronous mini-batch SGD [18] training with $batch\_size = 6144$ and data parallelism on 8 NVIDIA Tesla

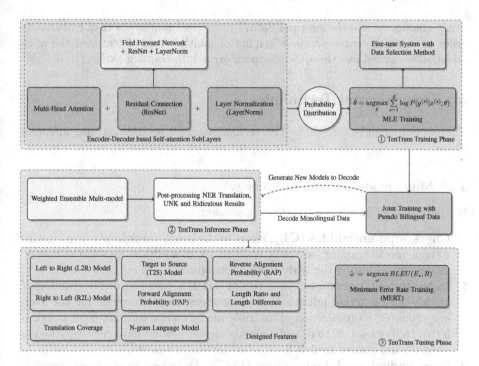

Fig. 1. An illustration of system architecture of TenTrans. This figure only describes the most basic sub-layer structure in the encoder and decoder. In addition, there is a sub-layer structure between the two. θ indicates model parameters being trained, and s indicates a training sample containing a source language x and a target language y. ω are the feature weight parameters being tuned by MERT. Ridiculous results mainly refer to translation results that are extremely long or short and clearly inconsistent with the source language.

P40 GPUs. We clip the gradient norm to 1.0 [19]. We apply residual dropout [20,21] with $P_{rd} = 0.3$ to avoid overfitting. In training, we don't just focus on the word with highest probability score, but let the likelihood calculation be smoother, so applying label smoothing [22] with $\epsilon_{ls} = 0.1$. All weight parameters are initialized according to uniform distribution in the interval $[-0.08, 0.08]$. We will early stop training [23] when there is no new maximum value of the validation BLEU for 10 consecutive save-points (saving every 10000 updates) and select the model with the highest BLEU score on the validation set.

We mainly optimize TenTrans system through three parts. First, through the first part of Fig. 1, multiple models are trained, and then the data selection method is used to continue to fine tune the system. Then, through the second part of Fig. 1, the combination of best multiple models is used to decode the monolingual corpus to generate pseudo-bilingual data, and then the pseudo-bilingual data is proportionally added to the training set to continue the training of the first stage, and these two phases are continuously iterated until convergence. Finally, the third stage, N-best rescoring phase, finds the best translation result among the translation candidates by designed multiple sets of features. In order to learn the corresponding weights of multiple sets of features, the optimization is carried out through minimum error rate training (MERT).

3   Experimental Techniques

This section mainly introduces the techniques used in training and inference phase.

3.1   Multi-model Fusion Technology

For multi-model fusion, we try three strategies:

1. **Checkpoint ensembles (CE),** refers to the last N checkpoints saved during a single model training, where N is set to 10. In addition, we add the best 10 models saved during the early stopping training.
2. **Independent parameter ensembles (IPE),** refers to firstly training N models with different initialization parameters, and then weighting the average probability distribution of multiple models when softmax layer is calculated. Here we set N to 6, and we make better models have relatively higher weights, and poorer models have relatively lower weights.
3. **Independent model ensembles (IME).** An independent model ensemble is a set of models, each of which has been assigned a weight. It is not necessary to perform calculating the probability distribution in the inference process. Our experimental results show that this method performs slightly lower than IPE method, but the advantage is that the decoding speed is the same as the single model decoding.

In this work, we use the checkpoint ensemble method to initially integrate each single model, and then use the independent parameter ensemble method to perform multi-model integration in the stage of generating the final result of the system. The independent model ensemble method is used to decode monolingual corpus to generate pseudo-bilingual data during joint training.

3.2   Fine-Tune System with Data Selection Method

In mainstream machine translation systems, network parameters are fixed after the training is finished. The same model will be applied to various test sentences. A very important problem with this approach is that it is difficult for a model to self-adapt to different sentences, especially when there is a big difference between the test set field and training set field. To alleviate this problem, [13] proposed to search similar sentences in the training data using the test sentence as a query, and then fine tune the NMT model using the retrieved training sentences for translating the test sentence. We follow the strategy of [13]. This method firstly learns the general model from the entire training corpus. Then, for each test sentence, we extract a small subset from the training data, consisting of sentence pairs whose source sides are similar to the testing sentence. The subset is used to fine tune the general model and get a specific model for every sentence. To calculate similarity between two sentences, we adopt Levenshtein distance, which calculates the minimum steps for converting a string to another string using insertion, deletion and substitution these operations. We firstly filter the training corpus by only considering those which have common words with the testing sentence, and then compute similarity with the filtered set. In order to speed up the calculation, we use the inverted index method.

3.3 Joint Training

This work tries two ways to use the monolingual corpus to enhance the training set: back-translation and joint training.

Back-Translation. This method do not need to change any training algorithm and model network structure, but training corpus is constructed directly through monolingual corpus. It uses the trained target-to-source NMT model to translate the target-side monolingual data, and then the translated source-side monolingual corpus is proportionally added to the training set to retrain the source-to-target NMT model. This method has been proven to be simple and effective, but it is easy to generate particularly outrageous translation results [10] in the process of back-translation, which will have a pretty bad impact on the quality of the training set.

Joint Training. This method refers to the use of the corresponding additional target side and source side monolingual data at the source-to-target (S2T) and the target-to-source (T2S) translation model, and jointly optimizing the two translation models through an iterative process. In each iteration, T2S model is used to generate pseudo bilingual data for S2T with target-side monolingual data, and S2T model is used to generate pseudo bilingual data for T2S with source-side monolingual data. This joint optimization approach enables the translation model in both directions to be improved, and generating better pseudo-training data to be added to the training set. Therefore, in the next iteration, it can train better model T2S model and S2T model, so on and so forth. The right part of the decoding phase of Fig. 1 outlines the iterative process of joint training. In addition, in order to solve the problem that back-translation often generates pseudo data with poor translation quality and thus affects model training, the generated training sentence pairs are weighted so that the negative impact of noisy translations can be minimized in joint training. Original bilingual sentence pairs are all weighted as 1, while the synthetic sentence pairs are weighted as the normalized corresponding model output probability. For the specific practice of joint training in this paper, see Algorithm 1.[2]

---

[2] Here $P'(x^{(t)}|y^{(t)})$ refers to translation probability of M_{t2s}^{ens} translating monolingual sentence $y^{(t)}$ to generate $x^{(t)}$, $P'(y^{(t)}|x^{(t)})$ refers to translation probability of M_{s2t}^{ens} translating monolingual sentence $x^{(t)}$ to generate $y^{(t)}$, $P(y^{(s)}|x^{(s)})$ denotes translation probability of $x^{(s)} \rightarrow y^{(s)}$ during training S2T model, and $P(x^{(s)}|y^{(s)})$ denotes translation probability of $y^{(s)} \rightarrow x^{(s)}$ during training T2S model.

In this work, we use joint training to enhance the training set in Chinese↔English and Uighur→Chinese translation system, and use back-translation method in Mongolian→Chinese and Tibetan→Chinese translation system.

Algorithm 1. Joint Training Algorithm in TenTrans System

Input: original bilingual data B, source monolingual data X_m, target monolingual data Y_m
Output: trained S2T models $M_{s2t}^i (i = 1 \cdots 6)$ and T2S models $M_{t2s}^i (i = 1 \cdots 6)$
1: Train 6 $M_{s2t}^i (i = 1 \cdots 6)$ and 6 $M_{t2s}^i (i = 1 \cdots 6)$ with different parameters
2: $n \Leftarrow 1$
3: **while** Not Converged **do**
4:     Integrate 6 $M_{s2t}^i (i = 1 \cdots 6)$ to generate M_{s2t}^{ens} with IME method
5:     Integrate 6 $M_{t2s}^i (i = 1 \cdots 6)$ to generate M_{t2s}^{ens} with IME method
6:     Use M_{t2s}^{ens} to generate pseudo-training data F_{t2s} by translating Y_m
7:     Use M_{s2t}^{ens} to generate pseudo-training data F_{s2t} by translating X_m
8:     New corpus to train $M_{s2t}^i (i = 1 \cdots 6)$, $C_{s2t} \Leftarrow n \times B + F_{t2s}$
9:     New corpus to train $M_{t2s}^i (i = 1 \cdots 6)$, $C_{t2s} \Leftarrow n \times B + F_{s2t}$
10:    $n \Leftarrow n + 1$
11:    Train M_{s2t}^i with $L(\theta_{s2t}) = \sum\limits_{s=1}^{S} \log P(y^{(s)}|x^{(s)}) + \sum\limits_{t=1}^{T} \log P(y^{(t)}|x^{(t)})P'(x^{(t)}|y^{(t)})$ using C_{s2t}^2
12:    Train M_{t2s}^i with $L(\theta_{t2s}) = \sum\limits_{s=1}^{S} \log P(x^{(s)}|y^{(s)}) + \sum\limits_{t=1}^{T} \log P(x^{(t)}|y^{(t)})P'(y^{(t)}|x^{(t)})$ using C_{t2s}^2
13: **end while**

3.4 Different Modeling Units

This work uses two subword modeling units to achieve open-vocabulary translation: Byte Pair Encoding (BPE) and mixed word/character segmentation. We use BPE[3] with 50K operations in both source side and target side of Chinese→English translation. In English→Chinese translation system, we use BPE with 50K operations in English source side, and use mixed word/character segmentation in Chinese target side. We keep the most frequent 60K Chinese words and split other words into characters. In post-processing step, we simply remove all the spaces. We use BPE with 16K operations in both side of Mongolian→Chinese translation.

3.5 NER Generalization Method

To alleviate poor translation performance of named entities, we first use the predefined tags to replace named entities in training set, for example, use $number for number, $time for time, $date for date, $psn for person name, $loc for location name, $org for organization name. Then the key to the problem is how to

---

[3] https://github.com/rsennrich/subword-nmt

identity these entities and classify them into corresponding types accurately. In order to solve this problem, we classify these entities into two types, one type that can be identified by rules, and the other type that can be identified by classification models. To decide whether an entity is a time, a number, or a date, we use finite automata (FA) [24] to identify them. Aiming at the names of people, location names, and organization names, we first use biLSTM-CRF[4] [25, 26] to train a Chinese sequence tagging model on "People's Daily 1998" data set and English sequence tagging model on CoNLL2003 data set, and then identify named entities at the source and target language side of the training set. Finally, we replace these entities in the training set with corresponding predefined tags to train a tagged NMT system.

In the test phase, we first convert these entities in the test sentence into corresponding predefined tags, and then directly using the tagged NMT system to translate the sentence. When a tag is generated at target side, we select the corresponding translation of the word in the source language side that has the highest alignment probability based attention probability with the same as tag type in target side. If the source side does not have the same type of tag, delete the current tag directly. In order to obtain the corresponding translation of each entity vocabulary, we obtain it in the phrase extraction stage in statistical machine translation (SMT) [27]. We extract a phase pair with one source word number from phrase table, and then use target side of the phase pair with highest frequency of occurrence as the translation of the word to construct a bilingual translation dictionary. Although this method has not greatly improved the BLEU evaluation metric, it is of great benefit to the readability of the translation result for human. We use UNK to represent out-of-vocabulary (OOV) words, and translate it in the same way as above.

4 Experimental Features

This section mainly focuses the features designed to help choose translation results which are closer to the way normal user expressions - that is, it focuses on the N-best rescoring phase. Several features designed in this work can be seen in the left part of third phase in Fig. 1.

4.1 Right to Left (R2L) Model

Since the current translation models all carry out modeling from left to right, there is a tendency for the prefix part of translation candidates to be higher quality than the suffix part [28]. In order to alleviate this problem of translation imbalance, we adopt a right-to-left translation modeling method. Two R2L modeling method are used in this work: the first is that only the target data is inversed, and the second is that both the target data and the source data are inversed. Then, two models, R2L model and R2L-both model were trained.

---

[4] https://github.com/guillaumegenthial/sequence_tagging

Finally, we also reverse the n-best lists and calculate the likelihood probability of each translation candidate given the source sentence using these two models. Each model mentioned above is integrated by training 6 models with different parameters.

4.2 Target to Source Model

Neural machine translation models often have the phenomena of missing translation, repeated translation, and obvious translation deviation [29]. In order to alleviate this problem, we use the target-to-source translation system to reconstruct the source-to-target translation results to the source sentence. This approach can make it very difficult to reproduce poor translation results to the source sentence, and the corresponding probability score will be low. Similarly, these models are all integrated by multiple models.

4.3 Alignment Probability

In order to express the degree of mutual translation between the translation candidate and source sentence at the lexical level, the lexical alignment probability feature is adopted. This paper uses two kinds of alignment probabilities, forward alignment probability and backward alignment probability. The forward alignment probability indicates the degree of alignment of source language vocabulary to the target language vocabulary, while the backward alignment probability indicates the degree of alignment of target language vocabulary to the source language vocabulary. We obtain the alignment score by *fast-align* toolkit[5] [30].

4.4 Length Ratio and Length Difference

In order to reflect the length ratio between source sentence and translation candidates, we designed the length ratio feature $R_{len} = Len(source)/Len(candidate)$ and the length difference feature $D_{len} = Len(source) - Len(candidate)$.

4.5 Translation Coverage

To reflect whether words in the source language sentences have been translated, we introduce translation coverage feature. This feature is calculated by adding one to the feature value if the source language words has been translated. We use the *fast-align* toolkit to count the top 50 target words with highest probability of aligning each source language word as the translation set of this source word.

---

[5] https://github.com/clab/fast_align.

4.6 *N*-gram Language Model

As a very powerful feature in statistical machine translation, language model is also used in TenTrans system. For English, the word-level 5-gram language model is trained on the mixing corpus of "News Crawl: articles from 2016" selected by newsdev2018 and English side of the training data. For Chinese, the character-level 5-gram language model is trained on the XMU[6]. This work uses KenLM[7] toolkit [31] to train *n*-gram language model.

4.7 Minimum Error Rate Training (MERT)

Obviously, some of the above features may be very powerful, while some of the effects are not particularly obvious. Therefore, we need to give each feature a corresponding weight. Our optimization goal is to find a set of feature weights that make the model score of translation candidates higher and the corresponding BLEU [32] score higher. Therefore, we use minimum error rate training method to learn the feature weights

$$
\begin{aligned}
\omega^* &= \underset{\omega}{\text{argmin}} \ Error(E_*, R) \\
&= \underset{\omega}{\text{argmin}} \ (1 - BLEU(E_*, R)) \\
&= \underset{\omega}{\text{argmax}} \ BLEU(E_*, R)
\end{aligned}
\tag{2}
$$

where ω^* indicates tuned weights, E_* indicates the best translation candidate for the source language and R represents the corresponding reference translation.

Table 1. Chinese↔English BLEU results on WMT2018 and CWMT2018

System	ZH→EN				EN→ZH			
	WMT18		CWMT18-Test		WMT18		CWMT18-Test	
	Valid.	Test	BLEU4-SBP	BLEU4	Valid.	Test	BLEU5-SBP	BLEU5
Baseline	23.32	-	-	-	33.06	-	-	-
+CE	24.06	-	-	-	33.84	-	-	-
+IPE	25.98	-	-	-	35.58	-	-	-
+back-translation	26.49	-	-	-	36.0	-	-	-
+joint training	26.96	-	-	-	36.51	-	-	-
+fine-tune	27.63	-	-	-	37.29	-	-	-
+NER genereralization	27.74	-	-	-	37.43	-	-	-
+reranking (beam size 12)	29.72	-	-	-	39.03	-	-	-
+reranking (beam size 100)	30.13	-	-	-	39.49	-	-	-
Final system	30.21	28.3	25.72	26.85	39.61	39.4	33.62	35.29

---

[6] http://nlp.nju.edu.cn/cwmt2018/resources.html.
[7] https://github.com/kpu/kenlm.

5   Experimental Settings and Results

In all experiments, we report case-sensitive, detokenized BLEU, using the NIST BLEU scorer[8]. For Chinese output, we split to characters using the script supplied for WMT18 before running BLEU. We used the official newsdev2018 as validation set. The Chinese sentences are segmented using NiuTrans [33] Segmenter[9]. For English sentences, we use the Moses [34] tokenizer[10]. For Mongolian sentences, we use original tokenization tools.

5.1   Chinese↔English System

We use all the training data of WMT2018 Chinese↔English translation tasks, firstly filtering out bilingual sentences with unrecognizable code, large length ratio difference, duplications and wrong language coding, then filtering out bilingual sentences with poor mutual translation rate by using *fast-align* toolkit. After data cleaning, 18.5 million sentence pairs remained. We used beam search with a beam size of 12, length penalty $\alpha = 0.8$ for Chinese→English system and length penalty $\alpha = 1.0$ for English→Chinese system. In order to recover the case information, we use Moses toolkit[11] to train SMT-based recaser on English corpus. In addition, we also use some simple rules to restore the case information of the results. The size of the Chinese vocabulary and English vocabulary is 64k and 50k respectively after BPE operation. Table 1 shows the Chinese↔English translation results on development set and test set of WMT2018 and test set of CWMT2018. Wherein reranking refers to multi-feature based rescore method mentioned above. Final system in Table 1 has slightly better performance than is seen in the previous experiment because we have manually written some rules. As can be seen from the Table 1, when we increase the size of n-best from 12 to 100, the performance is improved by 0.41 BLEU after reranking based on multiple features.

5.2   Mongolian→Chinese System

We use all the training data of Mongolian→Chinese translation task, filtering out bilingual data with the same process as Chinese↔English. After pre-processing, there are 190K high-quality parallel bilingual corpus. Afterwards, a high-quality parallel corpus is used to train the Chinese→Mongolian translation system, and then using this system to back-translate the XMU data set, and finally generating 1 million pseudo-parallel corpus after filtering. We used IMU-dev-mnzh-CWMT2018 as development set, and copied the 1001 source sentences into 4

---

[8] https://github.com/moses-smt/mosesdecoder/blob/master/scripts/generic/mteval-v13a.pl.

[9] http://www.niutrans.com/niutrans/NiuTrans.ch.html#download.

[10] https://github.com/moses-smt/mosesdecoder/blob/master/scripts/tokenizer/tokenizer.perl.

[11] https://github.com/moses-smt/mosesdecoder/blob/master/scripts/recaser/train-recaser.perl.

copies, making them correspond to the 4 reference translations one by one. In addition to using one sentence one model method, we use 190K high-quality data to fine-tune the model. We used beam search with a beam size of 12 and length penalty $\alpha = 1.5$. Table 2 shows the Mongolian→Chinese translation results on development set of CWMT2018.

Table 2. Mongolian→Chinese BLEU results on CWMT2018

System	BLEU4	BLEU5
Baseline	37.58	32.60
+fine-tune	40.04	34.75
+CE	41.16	35.65
+IPE	43.41	37.98
+reranking (beam size 12)	44.06	38.51
+reranking (beam size 50)	46.17	41.22

6   Conclusion

This paper describes TencentFmRD neural machine translation for CWMT2018. In training phase, we report five experimental techniques including multi-model fusion, joint training, fine-tune system with data selection method, different modeling units and NER generalization method. In the rescoring phase, we designed multiple features to ensure that candidates which are more likely to be produced by users are as close as possible to the top of n-best lists. We also reported the motivation of each designed feature. Our English↔ Chinese and Mongolian→Chinese systems achieve a stable performance improvement.

References

1. Cho, K., Merrienboer, B., Gulcehre, C., Bougares, F., Schwenk, H., Bengio, Y.: Learning phrase representations using RNN encoder-decoder for statistical machine translation. In: EMNLP (2014)
2. Sutskever, I., Vinyals, O., Le, Q.V.: Sequence to sequence learning with neural networks. In: Advances in Neural Information Processing Systems, pp. 3104–3112 (2014)
3. Bahdanau, D., Cho, K., Bengio, Y.: Neural machine translation by jointly learning to align and translate. In: Proceedings of ICLR (2014)
4. Sennrich, R., Haddow, B., Birch, A.: Edinburgh neural machine translation systems for WMT 16. In: Association for Computational Linguistics, Berlin, Germany (2016)
5. Wu, Y., et al.: Google's neural machine translation system: bridging the gap between human and machine translation. CoRR abs/1609.08144 (2016)

6. Vaswani, A., et al.: Attention is all you need. In: Advances in Neural Information Processing Systems, pp. 5998-6008 (2017)
7. Sennrich, R., Haddow, B., Birch, A.: Neural machine translation of rare words with subword units. In: Proceedings of ACL (2016)
8. Luong, M., Manning, C.D.: Achieving open vocabulary neural machine translation with hybrid word-character models. In: Proceedings of ACL (2016)
9. Sennrich, R., Haddow, B., Birch, A.: Improving neural machine translation models with monolingual data. In: Proceedings of ACL (2016)
10. Zhang, Z., Liu, S., Li, M., Zhou, M., Chen, E.: Joint training for neural machine translation models with monolingual data. In: Association for the Advancement of Artificial Copyright Intelligence (2018)
11. Och, F.J.: Minimum error rate training in statistical machine translation. In: Proceedings of the 41st Annual Meeting on Association for Computational Linguistics-Volume 1. Association for Computational Linguistics, pp. 160–167 (2003)
12. Wang, Y., et al.: Sogou neural machine translation systems for WMT 17. In: Proceedings of the Second Conference on Machine Translation, pp. 410–415 (2017)
13. Li, X., Zhang, J., Zong, C.: One sentence one model for neural machine translation. CoRR abs/1609.06490 (2016)
14. Chiang, D., DeNeefe, S., Chan, Y.S., Ng, H.T.: Decomposability of translation metrics for improved evaluation and efficient algorithms. In: Proceedings of the Conference on Empirical Methods in Natural Language Processing, Association for Computational Linguistics, pp. 610–619 (2008)
15. He, K., Zhang, X., Ren, S., Sun, J.: Deep residual learning for image recognition. In: Proceedings of the IEEE Conference on Computer Vision and Pattern Recognition, pp. 770–778 (2016)
16. Ba, J.L., Kiros, J.R., Hinton, G.E.: Layer normalization. arXiv preprint arXiv:1607.06450 (2016)
17. Kingma, D.P., Ba, J.: Adam: a method for stochastic optimization. arXiv preprint arXiv:1412.6980 (2014)
18. Dean, J., et al.: Large scale distributed deep networks. In: Advances in Neural Information Processing Systems, pp. 1223–1231 (2012)
19. Pascanu, R., Mikolov, T., Bengio, Y.: On the difficulty of training recurrent neural networks. In: International Conference on Machine Learning, pp. 1310–1318 (2013)
20. Zaremba, W., Sutskever, I., Vinyals, O.: Recurrent neural network regularization. In: Proceedings of ICLR (2014)
21. Srivastava, N., Hinton, G., Krizhevsky, A., Sutskever, I., Salakhutdinov, R.: Dropout: a simple way to prevent neural networks from overfitting. J. Mach. Learn. Res. 15(1), 1929–1958 (2014)
22. Szegedy, C., Vanhoucke, V., Ioffe, S., Shlens, J., Wojna, Z.: Rethinking the inception architecture for computer vision. In: Proceedings of the IEEE Conference on Computer Vision and Pattern Recognition, pp. 2818–2826 (2016)
23. Sennrich, R., et al.: The University of Edinburgh's neural MT systems for WMT17. arXiv preprint arXiv:1708.00726 (2017)
24. Thatcher, J.W., Wright, J.B.: Generalized finite automata theory with an application to a decision problem of second-order logic. Math. Syst. Theory 2(1), 57–81 (1968)
25. Lample, G., Ballesteros, M., Subramanian, S., Kawakami, K., Dyer, C.: Neural architectures for named entity recognition. arXiv preprint arXiv:1603.01360 (2016)
26. Huang, Z., Xu, W., Yu, K.: Bidirectional LSTM-CRF models for sequence tagging. arXiv preprint arXiv:1508.01991 (2015)

27. Koehn, P., Knight, K.: U.S. Patent No. 7,624,005. Washington, DC: U.S. Patent and Trademark Office (2009)
28. Liu, L., Utiyama, M., Finch, A., Sumita, E.: Agreement on target-bidirectional neural machine translation. In: Proceedings of the 2016 Conference of the North American Chapter of the Association for Computational Linguistics: Human Language Technologies, pp. 411–416 (2016)
29. Tu, Z., Liu, Y., Shang, L., Liu, X., Li, H.: Neural machine translation with reconstruction. In: AAAI, pp. 3097–3103 (2017)
30. Dyer, C., Chahuneau, V., Smith, N.A.: A simple, fast, and effective reparameterization of IBM model 2. In: Association for Computational Linguistics (2013)
31. Heafield, K.: KenLM: faster and smaller language model queries. In: Proceedings of the Sixth Workshop on Statistical Machine Translation. Association for Computational Linguistics, pp. 187–197 (2011)
32. Papineni, K., Roukos, S., Ward, T., Zhu, W.J.: BLEU: a method for automatic evaluation of machine translation. In: Proceedings of the 40th Annual Meeting on Association for Computational Linguistics. Association for Computational Linguistics, pp. 311–318 (2002)
33. Xiao, T., Zhu, J., Zhang, H., Li, Q.: NiuTrans: an open source toolkit for phrase-based and syntax-based machine translation. In: Proceedings of the ACL 2012 System Demonstrations. Association for Computational Linguistics, pp. 19–24 (2012)
34. Koehn, P., et al.: Moses: Open source toolkit for statistical machine translation. In: Proceedings of the 45th Annual Meeting of the ACL on Interactive Poster and Demonstration Sessions. Association for Computational Linguistics, pp. 177–180 (2007)

Author Index

Printed in the United States
By Bookmasters